The Literary Manager's Toolkit

The Literary Manager's Toolkit is a clear and comprehensive guide to the role of the literary manager in theatre and beyond, focusing on the key skills, networks, and processes that underpin a successful career in this and associated roles.

This book outlines the tasks and responsibilities of a literary manager in the selection, development, and production of new plays. In the first part, it outlines the how, when, and why of the literary manager's main activities, equipping the reader with everything that they will need when approaching this role's central challenges. The second part provides a selection of practical, accessible, and easy-to-follow materials and workshop suggestions for literary managers who will work with playwrights as they develop their creative writing and dramaturgy skills.

This is the go-to resource for the working professional literary manager or dramaturg, and for students on dramaturgy courses in theatre degree programmes.

Dr Sue Healy, from Ireland, is the literary manager at the Finborough Theatre and a full-time lecturer in creative writing for stage and screen at the University of Lincoln. She is also a playwright.

The Focal Press Toolkit Series

Regardless of your profession, whether you're a Stage Manager or Stagehand, The Focal Press Toolkit Series has you covered. With all the insider secrets, paperwork, and day-to-day details that you could ever need for your chosen profession or specialty, these books provide you with a one-stop-shop to ensure a smooth production process.

The Stage Manager's Toolkit, 3rd edition
Templates and Communication Techniques to Guide Your Theatre Production from First Meeting to Final Performance
Laurie Kincman

The Lighting Supervisor's Toolkit
Collaboration, Interrogation, and Innovation toward Engineering Brilliant Lighting Designs
Jason E. Weber

The Assistant Lighting Designer's Toolkit, 2nd edition
Anne E. McMills

The Projection Designer's Toolkit
Jeromy Hopgood

The Scenic Charge Artist's Toolkit
Tips, Templates, and Techniques for Planning and Running a Successful Paint Shop in the Theatre and Performing Arts
Jennifer Rose Ivey

The Costume Designer's Toolkit
The Process of Creating Effective Design
Holly Poe Durbin

The Literary Manager's Toolkit
A Practical Guide for the Theatre
Sue Healy

For more information about this series, please visit: https://www.routledge.com/The-Focal-Press-Toolkit-Series/book-series/TFPTS

The Literary Manager's Toolkit
A Practical Guide for the Theatre

Sue Healy

LONDON AND NEW YORK

Designed cover image: Photographer Benjamin Graham for the Criterion New Writing program

First published 2023
by Routledge
4 Park Square, Milton Park, Abingdon, Oxon OX14 4RN

and by Routledge
605 Third Avenue, New York, NY 10158

Routledge is an imprint of the Taylor & Francis Group, an informa business

© 2023 Sue Healy

The right of Sue Healy to be identified as author of this work has been asserted in accordance with sections 77 and 78 of the Copyright, Designs and Patents Act 1988.

All rights reserved. No part of this book may be reprinted or reproduced or utilised in any form or by any electronic, mechanical, or other means, now known or hereafter invented, including photocopying and recording, or in any information storage or retrieval system, without permission in writing from the publishers.

Trademark notice: Product or corporate names may be trademarks or registered trademarks, and are used only for identification and explanation without intent to infringe.

British Library Cataloguing-in-Publication Data
A catalogue record for this book is available from the British Library

ISBN: 9781032005140 (hbk)
ISBN: 9781032004624 (pbk)
ISBN: 9781003174523 (ebk)

DOI: 10.4324/9781003174523

Typeset in Times New Roman and Helvetica
by codeMantra

Figure 0.1 Donald Howarth at the Tyrone Guthrie Centre.

Dedicated to the memory of Donald Howarth (1931–2020), playwright, director, literary manager at the Royal Court Theatre 1975–1976, mentor of playwrights, and much-missed friend.

Contents

Foreword by Suzanne Bell — xi
Acknowledgements — xv
Introduction — 1

Part 1 — 7

Chapter 1: An evolving and elusive job description — 9

What a literary manager does 9
The paths into literary management 14
Locating the literary manager on theatre's managerial tree 17
Compensation for the literary manager 18
A potted history of the literary manager 20

Chapter 2: Attracting unsolicited scripts — 27

Encouraging the receipt of unsolicited scripts 28
Advising writers on what to submit 29
Advising writers on how to submit 32
Informing the writer of what happens next 36

Chapter 3: Systems, structures, and approaches — 39

The day-to-day operations of a literary department 39
Reading and assessing unsolicited scripts 42
Common approaches and procedures 42
Responding to the writer – unsolicited scripts 45
Assessing and responding to solicited scripts 47

*Sourcing solicited scripts and spotting
   playwrights of note   49*
Agents   51

Chapter 4: Dramaturgy 53

A history of dramaturgy   54
Dramaturgy today   56
Paths into dramaturgy   58
*The specific responsibilities of a
   dramaturge   60*

Chapter 5: Supporting and nurturing new writers 67

A pastoral role   67
A view from a playwright   69
Ways to mentor writers   78
Organising workshops   79
Running up a writers group   80
Start a social group linked to your venue   81
Hold industry talks   82
Obtaining funding for events   84
*The importance of clarity and managing
   expectations   86*
Funding mentorship   86
A seed commission   89
Writers residencies   91
Life advice   105

Chapter 6: Diversity and inclusion 109

Understanding your theatre's culture   109
Institutional habitus   110
Breaking down barriers   114
Check your lens and filters   116

Chapter 7: The issue of pay 121

*A consideration of the challenges facing
   a fringe theatre: to pay or not to pay
   readers   121*
A case study   122

Chapter 8: Life after literary management   133

    Next steps   133

PART 2   135

    The literary manager as teacher   135

Suggested workshops   137

    Workshop 1: Getting started   137
    Workshop 2: Getting Started II   139
    Workshop 3: Giving meaning   141
    Workshop 4: Shaping story   145
    Workshop 5: Developing characters   149
    Workshop 6: Active dialogue   153
    Workshop 7: Setting – genre   155
    Workshop 8: Dialogue   157
    Workshop 9: Universal stories   159

Useful teaching materials   161

    Stephen Jeffreys' nine stories   161
    Questions   161
    Answers   162
    A story scaffold   162
    Bonus activity using the story scaffold   163
    Know your story   164
    Transitive verbs   166

Bibliography   169
Index   171

Foreword

I have always found the role of literary manager challenging to define. Across my 20-year career, I have had six different job titles – including literary manager – for essentially the same job. People don't always know what we do and, to be honest, it can be hard to explain. I try to abbreviate it to "anything to do with writers and plays" but that doesn't do justice to the myriad of elements to the role. Furthermore, people come to this position through so many different routes, carving out their own distinctive approach. This book is an invaluable resource for exploring and defining the position more clearly.

For me, the role of literary manager is essentially a facilitative one, meaning that we serve, challenge, and drive an artist's vision. It can be difficult to put personal taste aside and it is important to be aware of our subjectivity. But I believe the skill and joy of the work is to investigate and endeavour to fulfil someone else's vision

Figure 0.2 The Interior of the Royal Exchange Theatre, Manchester.

and artistic ambition. I treasure the detective work of deep dives into different worlds and contrasting lives. It allows me to open up new areas of interest and discover distinctive voices in the work. The way we enable the artist to remain true to their vision is through facilitating an environment in which they feel safe and held to be vulnerable and playful. There is nothing more rewarding than seeing an artist find a way to articulate their ideas, see their imagination soar, and witness an audience of hundreds share a connection to their work.

At the heart of the appointment is also the imperative to ask questions and listen deeply. From the outset, we ask questions about how we might be most useful to a project, a process, or the journey of an artist. What systems do we need to create to fulfil the work's ambition and to ensure writers feel empowered to share their work? How do we put in place an infrastructure that enables us to respond to work in a way that is useful to both the organisation and the artist? How is the theatre a home for a diverse range of people? I find myself thinking about the space, the community the work is serving, who the work might reach, and the conversation that the work is having with that audience and the wider theatre cosmology.

Ultimately, there are certainly common features that literary managers share – most importantly, a deep love of theatre, playwrights, scripts, and stories. They need a voracious appetite to read and discover work, building an encyclopaedic knowledge of plays and a keen interest in the movements of theatre and the arts more broadly. Prizing the role of the playwright is essential. And a dedication to the conviction that all plays were new plays once and that we must support new work onto our stages.

We are always searching for the elusive euphoria that comes with reading something that is really working. I can still remember the first time I read the early drafts of new plays that eventually went into production. At the crack of dawn (a literary manager never gets to the bottom of the script pile), on a red-eye flight from New York to Manchester (long journeys can be a great time to give over to reading), and in my Mum's back garden (grabbing any spare time I could find). In those moments I remember my breath catching, my heart racing, my grip of the script tightening as I realised something in the playwright's voice and creativity demanded to be heard and seen in front of a live audience.

The way I work as a literary manager has been impacted by the many inspirational playwrights, directors, dramaturges, and theatre makers I have learnt from over the years. I am delighted that this book now explores, defines, and celebrates such a rewarding and essential role in theatre.

Suzanne Bell
New Writing Associate,
Royal Exchange Theatre, Manchester

Acknowledgements

This book stands on the shoulders of theatre giants, be they dramaturges, literary managers, theatre industry workers, or playwrights. In the first instance, I must thank all the literary managers and dramaturges, retired and current, who shared their thoughts and insights with me and gave me their precious time when I was compiling this book: Nickie Miles-Wildin, Tommo Fowler, Rebecca Mairs, Suzanne Bell, Gavin Kostick, Fleur Hebditch, Chris Campbell, and Harriet Devine. I am equally thankful to Mark Holme of the Manchester Performing Arts Group who noted a need for a book on theatre literary management and insisted I was the one to write it, providing all the crucial early encouragement on this journey. I am also thankful for the further information provided by translator William Gregory.

I am grateful too for the playwrights who candidly shared their experiences of working with literary managers, your insight has been enormously informative Simon Stephens and Simon Farquhar. I am indebted to the experience I have gained as literary manager at London's Finborough Theatre, not least the in-house, on-hand training generously given by its artistic director, Neil McPherson and the above-and-beyond help I receive daily from the deputy literary manager, Rhys Hayes. Thanks also to playwright Carmen Nasr with whom I ran the Finborough Forum for four years. All the know-how I share here is rooted from this support and education.

I extend thanks to those who have indirectly contributed to this guide, via their own workshops and publications, not least the late playwright and dramaturge Stephen Jeffreys who was responsible for teaching the art of playwriting to a generation of writers and theatre-makers. Heartfelt thanks also to that noted supporter of writers Greg Mosse, who has been characteristically generous in helping me put this guide together. I am likewise indebted to the late screenwriter and mentor Gill Dennis, whose insight on narrative approaches also informs this study. Further gratitude is expressed to those from whom I've learned a great deal about this industry, about being a literary manager, and a playwright: Graham Whybrow, Jim Nolan, and the late Donald Howarth.

I wish to thank my colleagues at the University of Lincoln: Professor Jason Whittaker, Dr Jacqueline Bolton, Dr James Hudson, Dr Guy Mankowski, Dr Chris Dows, Dr Sarah Stovell, Dr Amy Lilwall, Rob Weston, and Daniele Pantano. Additional heartfelt thanks to Professor Mark O'Thomas, Dr Nicholas Holden and Dr Harry Derbyshire of the University of Greenwich for their editorial work on my *Comparative Drama* article regarding payment in fringe theatres, which I draw upon in this guide. And thank you to all my students, who keep my teaching skills finely honed and provide daily opportunities for me to practice and improve my craft. Appreciation also to my agent, Jasmine Daines-Pilgrem. And finally, thanks to my parents Aiden and Paula, for everything.

This book is designed for students of theatre studies, teachers and lecturers in theatre studies, theatre industry workers, and playwrights, and all those with an interest in theatre and its operations and managerial architectures. The guide is the child of my years as a teacher, playwright, and literary manager. I write this study in celebration of the multi-talented plate-spinner and resident guru that is the literary manager – long may you guide, advise, mentor, organise, smooth over, settle down, and direct the lost. Guide on you shining shepherds.

Introduction

This book is an introductory guide to the role of the theatre literary manager. Though a key figure in many British and Irish playhouses today, a literary manager's responsibilities are little understood beyond the theatre industry. Indeed, even within the theatre world, only a small minority of industry workers can accurately describe what their literary manager actually does. This book addresses all the fuzziness surrounding the position of literary manager by exploring all the aspects of this mysterious job, revealing the role's purpose within the theatre in a simple and accessible manner, and examining the extent of and the reasons for the variance in job description.

This guide proceeds to offer practical and useful advice for those launching or considering a career in this profession and provides a clearer understanding of the literary manager's role for those working elsewhere in the theatre industry, for all students of theatre, and for those simply interested in the architecture of the theatre world. For this purpose, the specific objectives of the literary manager are explored and explained with clarity. In addition to sharing my own experience, much of the guidance included here has been elicited from current and former literary managers who have generously provided interviews and detailed here their own techniques and approaches. Helpful strategies are laid out. There is consideration of administrative responsibilities and paperwork, and thought is given to how one might negotiate typical obstacles, and how to develop those all-important communication skills.

Confusion surrounding the responsibilities of the literary manager is understandable as we will discover, but it is problematic. As Jacqueline Bolton argues in her thesis Demarcating Dramaturgy, "a conflation of dramaturgy with literary management… reduces the multiplicity of functions held by contemporary literary manager."[1] The cloudiness surrounding the job description of the literary manager is due in large part to the fact that this role is a relatively new introduction to these islands and its remit tends to vary from theatre to theatre, along with the title. One theatre's literary manager can have exactly the same duties as another theatre's dramaturge, or their resident dramatist, or creative reader, or commissions manager, or literary coordinator, or literary associate – and a blend of some of these roles is particularly common in regional theatres. Fleur Hebditch, who is titled the "assistant producer and literary coordinator" at the Stephen Joseph Theatre, Scarborough, provides this example:

> I am the only person in the literary department, so in effect, I do what a literary manager does. Part of my week is spent producing and programming and part of it is spent on the literary. This situation is quite common in regional theatres where perhaps the theatre cannot afford to have a full-time literary department, so they don't have a full-time literary manager but have someone who deals with all the tasks a literary manager will normally handle and have a different, if similar, title. I wear two hats in this theatre as I'm also and involved in producing, but the crossover is often beneficial.[2]

Conversely, a single theatre can have a literary manager, a dramaturge, and a literary associate – all with separate and specific obligations.[3] As a rule of thumb, those described as a literary manager tend to be employed by building-based theatre companies, and in a full-time or part-time capacity, whereas a dramaturge is frequently freelance and often contracted for a single production. One helpful way to remember this difference is that a literary manager might hire a dramaturge for a new production

Figure I.1 Stephen Joseph Theatre, Scarborough.

at their theatre, but a dramaturge hiring a literary manager would be highly unusual. Chris Campbell, former literary manager at the Royal Court Theatre, explains:

> Dramaturgy is an aspect of the literary manager's job, but it is not their sole focus. The dramaturge is engaged with analysing and advancing the text, the literary manager does this, but also has more broad and wide ranging responsibilities. That is how it is in this country, although I am aware that in Germany, for example, a dramaturge's role might involve aspects of literary management. As a literary manager you might hire a dramaturge to work on a play your theatre has programmed, perhaps because it is not one for which you feel you could provide the necessary dramaturgy. You would never however, hire a freelance literary manager. You are running the literary department, maintaining and developing your theatre's relationship with writers, agents and the artistic director and keeping an eye on trends. The Literary Manager's Job is more complex and far-reaching.[4]

Figure I.2 Chris Campbell.

Rebecca Mairs, literary manager at Belfast's Lyric Theatre, concurs with Campbell's take on this difference:

> There is definitely more admin involved for the literary manager. In many ways, it's an administrative role. You are also involved to some extent in marketing, in creative learning and in providing and designing website content and overseeing initiatives. A dramaturge is a member of the creative team, like a choreographer. The literary manager will also be a dramaturge, but not exclusively. As a dramaturge, you are in the rehearsal room with the writer.
>
> There are definitely times when I as a literary manager would consider hiring a dramaturge, if the project was one I didn't feel I could advise on. You need to have the right dramaturge for a project.[5]

As Campbell and Mairs highlight, a literary manager's duties will normally incorporate dramaturgy, but in addition to other administrative and managerial responsibilities. As Hebditch phrases it: "The role of the literary manager encapsulates dramaturgy, it umbrellas it, but the literary manager role is more complex and can involve aspects of production."[6]

As this guidebook explores, the literary manager's role usually spans beyond the text. They are normally engaged in fostering, advising, advocating for, and empowering emerging talent. In contrast, dramaturges tend to be more focused on the play-at-hand, rather than on the long-term career of the playwright. There is a great deal of overlap and grey areas between all these job titles, certainly. Due to the different interpretations of the job, this book does not and cannot provide an incontrovertible definition of the literary manager's responsibilities, rather it explores the different understandings of the job, outlines what the literary manager's work *usually* involves, and provides practical and helpful advice on dealing with all these aspects of the job. For the purposes of simplicity and to save confusion, this guide tends to refer to all the aforementioned job titles collectively as the 'literary manager.' Here, the usual responsibilities that a literary manager will have are mapped, as are approaches and strategies for navigating these duties.

Although the position of literary manager is recent in Britain and Ireland, mainland European theatres and German theatres in particular have long housed a figure dealing with play development since the late 18th century. Today, across continental Europe these specific theatre professionals are most often tasked with the dramaturgical research and consultancy on productions of established plays, rather than seeking out and fostering new playwrights. In other words, continental literary managers are closer to the definition of the dramaturge. This guide examines why, how, and to what extent since its arrival in Britain in the mid-20th century, the position of the literary manager has diverged from its more dramaturgy-predicated roots in Europe.

Adding to all this ambiguity regarding the job, in Hollywood and the international film world, a 'literary manager' tends to refer to the person who represents scripts in the way an agent might represent an actor. This film-world description is NOT the literary management role outlined in this book. Within the theatrescape of North America, however, the position of literary manager exists, but as Campbell explains: "It's often given a different label. The Manhattan Theatre Club has a department that operates as a literary department, though they may call it something else. Also, the Atlantic Theatre."[7] Additionally, in North America, the literary manager is the title of a job that can have more in common with that of the theatre manager. This guide pertains only to the responsibilities of a literary manager in theatre as the term is generally used and understood within the theatre industry of Britain and Ireland.

It is safe to state that the cornerstone of literary management in Britain and Ireland remains writer development. On these islands, the literary manager will instigate and oversee development schemes and talent spotting initiatives and events and will provide all manner of guidance for emerging playwrights. Indeed, literary managers will even be involved in advising and directing writers in a manner that can border on the pastoral. Additionally, they are frequently tasked with designing, creating, and encouraging a favourable environment in which new writing can flourish and bloom under the auspices of their theatre. Occasionally, the literary manager's reach will touch community engagement, perhaps even fund raising, marketing, and advertising. There may be involvement in production. For the most part, however, the attention of the literary manager will be playwright focused.

This study provides an overview of the job as outlined above and in this way, unpicks what is broadly understood by the term literary manager today, considers what one might reasonably expect someone in this post to provide, and what they are unlikely to deliver. Here, we explore the various challenges facing literary managers at the present time and consider effective solutions and tools used to carry out the duties most effectively. With its focus on an easy-to-use practicality, this guide should become the go-to book for the student, for those considering, or launching, a career in literary management, and more broadly for those who are new to the world of theatre and keen to understand the machinations and dynamics of the industry.

I have held the position of literary manager at the London's Finborough Theatre for over five years. I am also a playwright, a screen and radio dramatist, an academic with a doctorate in theatre history, and a tutor of and lecturer in dramatic writing – and am drawing on my decades-long experience in all the above, in writing and compiling this guide.

I hope this book will also go some way to de-mystifying the job description of the literary manager and provide a map and a comprehensive yet accessible account of the role's responsibilities and its pivotal function within the world of theatre.

Sue Healy

London, May 21st, 2022

NOTES

1. Bolton, J. *Demarcating Dramaturgy, Mapping Theory onto Practice* (2011). https://etheses.whiterose.ac.uk/3315/.
2. Fleur Hebditch interview with Sue Healy via Zoom, July 22nd, 2021.
3. In February 2001, Ben Barnes the then artistic director at the Abbey Theatre (Ireland's national theatre), announced a major structural overhaul of that theatre's literary department. It was reported that the position of dramaturge was to be dissolved, and the literary manager, Judy Friel, was to concentrate on what he referred to as 'the pragmatic side of literary management.' Barnes also announced a new position of 'commissions manager,' or a figure who was to manage commissions, recommend new commissions and scout for talent.
4. Chris Campbell was literary manager at the Royal Court Theatre 2010–2019, and previously deputy literary manager at the National Theatre. He is also a translator and actor. (Interviewed by Sue Healy, London, July 21, 2021).
5. Sue Healy's interview with Rebecca Mairs, via Zoom, August 10, 2021.
6. Fleur Hebditch interview with Sue Healy via Zoom, July 22, 2021.
7. Chris Campbell interviewed by Sue Healy, London, July 21, 2021.

PART 1

CHAPTER 1

An evolving and elusive job description

WHAT A LITERARY MANAGER DOES

A literary manager is at the core of the artistic activity of a theatre, and most literary managers are usually associated with theatres focused on new writing. Indeed, they are often the first point of contact for emerging playwrights. Literary managers frequently also work as a dramaturge within their own theatre, though as has been revealed in the introduction, this single aspect is rarely the sole focus of their job.

In Britain and Ireland today, a literary manager tends to operate as an entity between a dramaturge, literary consultant, and artistic manager. So, depending on the institution, they will have some programming, managerial, or even marketing responsibilities, in addition to their talent development duties.

It is challenging to nail down specific tasks commonly carried out by *all* literary managers as the position is in such a state of flux. Indeed, a change in responsibilities can even occur as a literary manager is *in situ*. Rebecca Mairs literary manager at Belfast's Lyric Theatre describes how her remit has evolved during her time.

> [The role of the literary manager at the Lyric] has actually changed quite a bit since I took the position in 2016. At that time, it was a newly-created job funded by the Arts Council of Northern Ireland. The funding was significantly geared towards developing new writing throughout Northern Ireland and we encouraged submissions from everyone. In reality, this lead to me being more the literary manager for all new writing in Northern Ireland and clearly such a situation drew heavily on time and

> resources and was untenable in the long term as I couldn't focus properly on my specific work at the Lyric. To counter this issue, we launched the New Playwriting Programme, a development initiative for writers from across the UK and the island of Ireland, which is administered within a specific time-frame. In this way, I can see that we are accessible for all new writers, but that I also have time to focus on the theatre.[1]

Despite inevitable changes in focus and the mission and objectives of the theatre, common responsibilities do begin to emerge. Hebditch, who works at the Stephen Joseph theatre in Scarborough details her literary responsibilities:

> I look after unsolicited scripts, manage the reports from volunteer readers, am engaged with talent development and I arrange events such as scratch nights and readings of new writing. I also give talks to external departments to students and visitors to the theatre. In many ways, this job is what the person makes it. I've learned from a recently found archive, largely of rejection letters, that there was in fact an initial literary department at the Stephen Joseph, overseen by Alan Ayckbourn, our then Artistic Director – it's been quite interesting to read through some of them from over 30 years ago. However, this was long gone by the time I arrived, so I had to build a literary department up again.[2]

Figure 1.1 Fleur Hebditch.

Script reading, supporting new writers, and representing the theatre also feature in Campbell's account of his experience of literary management. Campbell worked as a deputy literary manager at the National Theatre before taking up the literary manager post at the Royal Court in 2010. He compares his experiences at both venues, and in both positions:

> At the National I was charged with establishing and maintaining relationships with writers. I attended meetings and was able to give my opinion on scripts to leading figures such as Nicholas Hytner and Katie Mitchell. In this way, I had agency and influence within a theatre for the first time. What changed for me was that at the Court, as Literary Manager, I had final responsibility. I had to say no to people. I quickly learned that I had to be very careful what I said to writers. If, for example, I said that I loved a play, a writer might understand that it was a commitment to programme the work. Writers often hear only what they want to hear. I had to learn to be clear, and honest, at all times. I also learned to champion work but to not to overdo it. Artistic directors tend not to like you saying, for example, "if you don't programme this I'll resign."[3]

Figure 1.2 The Royal Court Theatre, Sloane Square, London.

Demonstrating that when it comes to literary management, there is always an exception to every rule, Gavin Kostick is in the unusual position of being a literary manager at a non-building-based theatre company. Ireland's Fishamble is a playwright-centred theatre company engaged in developing and producing new writing, fostering writers, and running related initiatives. Fishamble focuses on works about Ireland or works by Irish writers. They also engage with multi-authored work and the broader spectrum of theatre. Kostick elaborates:

> We see ourselves as being at the heart of new Irish writing and we produce new work from all over the Island of Ireland and tour throughout the country and internationally. Additionally, we run developmental workshops for plays of promise and work closely with the Irish Theatre Institute and the Dublin Fringe.[4]

Figure 1.3 The Ha'penny Bridge, Dublin.

The services Fishamble's literary department provides certainly leans into dramaturgical support, but it also reaches beyond dramaturgy. Kostick helpfully details the specific responsibilities of his position:

I manage the company's literary affairs. It's a part-time role, 20 hours per week. It's unusual in that I'm a non-venue based literary manager. It's a paid position, and not all literary managers are. Like many others in this industry I wear a number of hats and balance this job with other responsibilities. I'm also a lecturer in dramaturgy at the Lír Academy, and I'm a playwright myself. At Fishamble, I'm responsible for ensuring that we read all plays that are sent to us, and that submissions and queries are responded to in a timely fashion. We cannot always offer a thorough consideration of all plays, due to time constraints, but we aim to provide some thoughts on the work and perhaps some developmental suggestions where possible. With our New Play Clinic, I provide dramaturgical support for 8–10 plays a year.

About 50% of what I do is admin and correspondence related, and the rest is dramaturgy and workshops.

I'm responsible for the tone of Fishamble because I'm often the first point of contact for playwrights. I try to ensure that we're perceived as friendly, professional, engaged and jargon-free. It's key that I communicate that we care deeply about new writing in Ireland. I work closely with Jim Culleton (the artistic director) on commissioning plays, and I liaise daily with our General Manager, Eva Scanlan.[5]

These interviews illustrate the broad spectrum of set-ups and environments in which the literary manager might operate. Their remit certainly varies company to company. However, it is possible to identify the following ubiquitous responsibilities:

- Identify emerging playwrights of talent
- Source new plays of note and promise
- Ascertain future theatre directions and trends
- Nurture and encourage potential in playwrights
- Advocate for the new writer
- Design initiatives and environments to facilitate and foster talent
- Oversee the dramaturgical development of works for production
- Manage the literary department
- Attend new plays in other venues

Playwright Simon Stephens succinctly summarises the literary manager's duties, as he has encountered in his long experience of dealing with the profession:

> [Literary managers are] employed to read plays and to identify plays that accord with the guiding artistic principles of their theatre. A literary manager needs to know what will accord with their theatre's programme. They also need to work with the writers they are excited by, to develop a relationship with them, to encourage, inspire, provoke them, engage them in conversation.[6]

THE PATHS INTO LITERARY MANAGEMENT

There is no set path into this profession, nor any qualifications that are entirely necessary, though there are essential traits. A theatre's literary manager should have a strong and demonstrably long-held interest in theatre and be well acquainted with a great variety and number of stage plays. It's imperative that a literary manager instinctively knows the difference between a great play and an also-ran, for example. It's characteristic of those in this position to be able to draw upon a broad and deep personal knowledge of the established dramatic canon, of contemporary plays, playwrights, and all current and past approaches to theatre-making. Some time spent as a reader of unsolicited and solicited scripts at a theatre's literary department would commonly feature on a candidate's CV, for example. Campbell describes here his path to the position of literary manager at the Royal Court:

> I was an actor for 10 years before I was invited to join the reading panel at the National Theatre, which involved assessing unsolicited scripts. I then became chair of the reading panel, the senior reader. I was subsequently invited to be the Deputy Literary Manager at the National, although at the time there was actually no Literary Manager, rather an associate director with responsibility for the literary department. Sometime after this, the Royal Court Theatre encouraged me to apply for the position of Literary Manager at Sloane Square.[7]

As Campbell's experience evidences, having many contacts within the theatre cosmology is additionally helpful when needing intel on opportunities for work as a literary manager. The track records of most applicants for a literary management position will show that they are already working in the industry – though not necessarily in a literary department. In fact, any experience in other areas of theatre, such as production and performance is advantageous. Hebditch elaborates:

> I was originally an actress in London. I left to start a family and we moved to Scarborough. I quickly got a job in the box office at the Stephen Joseph Theatre. In this way, I got to know the theatre and they could see what my skills were, and my knowledge. The associate director at the time began to ask me to help organise events and I was then approached by the artistic director to assist in planning the literary evening for the 60th anniversary of the theatre. I discovered that literary work was something I really wanted to do. It's interesting that I was recently in a room of people who were all working in literary management and only one of us had studied dramaturgy. So, there is not really a conventional route into the profession. I do think actors get a good training in dramaturgy however, particularly in how they might approach a script.[8]

Meanwhile, Mairs reveals how she navigated a circuitous route into a literary management position, from another arts sector, film:

> For a start, I don't have an academic background in theatre, like many literary managers will have. I started out very interested in film. I studied English Literature at university for my BA and then an MA in medieval studies at Queens University, Belfast. My interest in film led to a course in making short films in Kilkenny, and then a job at Northern Ireland Screen in the script department as a development executive in page-to-production. I read hundreds of scripts and gained a lot of story knowledge and experience, but realised after a year that this wasn't leading anywhere in particular. In Northern Ireland at that time, there wasn't the film industry that might have supported my career. The BBC were mainly interested in comedy and there wasn't the drama interest that there is now. I heard that the Lyric were keen to set up a talent development scheme and I applied for it, thinking I wasn't going to get it, not having a background in theatre. I met with [the Lyric's artistic director] Jimmy Faye and we got on well. I was offered the position. In many ways, I had to shape the role according the needs of the community and the theatre. Because of my background, I know I wouldn't necessarily favour someone with an MA in dramaturgy if looking for someone to work in a literary department. I would lean more towards reading experience.[9]

Figure 1.4 Greg Mosse, Criterion New Writing Program, Financed by the Criterion Theatre Trust.

Whatever their entry point, it's advisable that the person in the literary manager's position has robust organisational and managerial qualities; can oversee schedules, problem solve, be resourceful, and work well under pressure. It's additionally preferable that they possess strong people skills. A talent for communication and encouragement, with generous side-helpings of compassion and empathy, are of exceptional benefit in this position, particularly as it often involves a pastoral element of counselling and advising playwrights on life choices. Good public speaking abilities are an additional and welcome asset when giving talks on your theatre's activities, or running workshops. And, as with most positions in a theatre, a sense of humour will go a long way.

Literary managers are often playwrights themselves, or actors, or theatre people who have been involved in production in some capacity. Also, as Mairs evidences, a literary manager can come quite smoothly from the world of film criticism or screenplay development, for example. I have met literary managers with an unrelated background in law, or fine art, or education – but all nonetheless have an evident and deep knowledge of and appreciation for theatre, in all its forms, and a nose for story. Having a background in other sectors that work with narrative development, would be a bonus, as Mairs advises:

> There would definitely be openings [in a literary department] for someone who has worked as a freelance dramaturg, or script editor, or as a development executive for theatre and film or even working in publishing. Clearly, there is a difference between theatre and film, but there are overlaps also and if you have a grounding in story, you have a transferable skill.

A qualification in theatre studies is not a requirement therefore, but a willingness and ability to quickly learn about all things theatre related, probably is. At the time of writing, there is no third-level course where one can study literary management *per se*; however, there are a small number of post-graduate courses that specialise in dramaturgy, playwriting, or criticism – areas related to the work of the literary manager:

> **BRITAIN**
>
> **MA Dramaturgy** Birkbeck, University of London, Central London http://www.bbk.ac.uk
> **MA Dramaturgy** Leeds Conservatoire, Leeds http://www.bbk.ac.uk
> **MA Dramaturgy/Writing for Performance** Goldsmiths, London http://www.gold.ac.uk
> **MLitt Playwriting and Dramaturgy** University of Glasgow http://www.gla.ac.uk
>
> **IRELAND**
>
> **MFA Playwriting** The Lír Academy, Trinity College Dublin http://www.thelir.ie[10]

LOCATING THE LITERARY MANAGER ON THEATRE'S MANAGERIAL TREE

The literary manager forms part of the managerial team of a theatre. The theatre tree is headed by the artistic director, with whom the literary manager will normally work quite closely and advise in regards to programming. In this sense, the literary manager will often be something of a deputy artistic director, particularly pertaining to the venue's artistic aims and functions. The literary manager will also be expected to liaise frequently with the director of a production and will have lesser involvement with designers, actors, or technicians – though the extent and limit of such involvement usually depend on the size of the theatre and to what extent the literary manager is also the theatre's resident dramaturge.

A literary manager, therefore, often has a foot in the managerial camp, the production camp and in the artistic camp and can be considered a conduit between all. By operating as a bridge between these departments, the literary manager will sometimes co-ordinate the flow of information from the artistic director to the writer, director, and production. When doing so, they will need to be constantly mindful and alert to ensuring the specific artistic intentions of the theatre are being met by all. Chris Campbell considers his time as literary manager at the Court and the literary manager's relationship with the artistic director, the writers, and the theatre:

> It's important to know what you're not – you're not a critic, or a teacher. You're not marking the script. You're focused on developing conversations with writers, reading work and finding what is right for the theatre and finding a way forward when you find potential. You must have a good relationship with your artistic director. You must respect each other and understand and respect each other's taste. Honesty is crucial, with writers and with your response to plays and in all your communication. Always be open to a manuscript. And try to read and respond in good time, though admittedly that is not always possible, you should at least try. Also, it's important to be aware of the power dynamic and be mindful that people may have ulterior motives for being nice to you, and that equally, you can't abuse your position. Never forget that and keep your ego in check.[11]

To summarise, you need many attributes to be a literary manager: a keen eye for talent, a knowledge of drama to rival an Oxford don, the organisational skills of a producer, the empathy of a social worker, a good sense of humour, a strong sense of the *zeitgeist*, and last but not least, the courage of your convictions.

COMPENSATION FOR THE LITERARY MANAGER

Figure 1.5 The Author Sue Healy, Literary Manager at The Finborough Theatre.

You can expect anything from zero (i.e. a voluntary position)[12] to earning around £45,000, which would be the top-paid literary manager position in the sector. Like all areas of the arts, theatre is not a well-paid industry. A very tiny number of people, such as producers, writers, or actors, can very, very occasionally make a financial killing certainly, but the vast majority of theatre workers will just about make a living – and the literary manager will always fall into the latter category, as Campbell explains:

> [Pay] very much depends on where you're working. Theatre is not very well paid in general. The Royal Court Theatre role would be the pinnacle of the profession, perhaps one of two highly respected positions in the country, and in terms of compensation you're looking at the low 40Ks. In more mid-ranking theatres it would be £22k-£28k, the equivalent perhaps of a trainee solicitor in their first year.[13]

No sane person would enter a career in literary management with a view to getting rich. However, one is likely to be well rewarded in terms of job satisfaction, as Kostick points out:

> Few jobs in theatre pay very well and people enter the profession for the love of it, rather than the money. Not many literary manager roles are paid and when they are, they are often part-time and usually need to be supported by other jobs in the industry in order to raise a family and pay and mortgage and the like. It's an enormously satisfying job however.[14]

Literary managers also enjoy status, and appreciation, as many writers will testify. Leading English playwright Simon Stephens offers his appraisal:

> I am so grateful to all the literary managers I've worked with, from Graham Whybrow through to Sarah Frankcom, who was then at the Royal Exchange, and later Chris Campbell and Ruth Little who both worked at the Royal Court. Without them I would not have a career. Graham and Sarah were particularly crucial to my early years, and I owe them a great deal.[15]

A POTTED HISTORY OF THE LITERARY MANAGER

In Britain and Ireland, today the definition of the term literary manager is not widely understood beyond the theatre industry, and indeed there remains confusion within. The specific responsibilities of the position of a literary manager at any British or Irish theatre will greatly depend on the needs and traditions of the particular institution. Some literary managers will be largely active and engaged in dramaturgy, others will have greater involvement in managing the theatre, overseeing administrative duties, launching and heading initiatives as well as scouting, fostering, and maintaining relationships with emerging and established playwrights. Although the literary manager may be engaged in many aspects of running a theatre, often depending on the size of the venue, they will likely be responsible for the reading and evaluation of scripts submitted to the theatre for consideration and/or advising the artistic director on programming.

In mainland Europe, and particularly Germany, the text-focused position of dramaturge has been associated with theatres since the latter half of the 18th century. Throughout the early to mid-20th century, British theatres, however, tended towards casually appointing industry professionals such as actors or playwrights to the role of reader or senior reader of solicited and unsolicited play scripts. Any dramaturgical support a playwright might receive for a new play was largely the responsibility of that play's director. It was the 1960s before an equivalent of the in-house dramaturge was introduced to these islands, the concept imported from Germany. But upon arrival in Britain, the job took its own distinct shape and title.

Renowned theatre critic Kenneth Tynan was the first theatre industry professional in Britain to be termed a literary manager.[16] This designation occurred when he accepted a literary advisory appointment at Britain's Royal National Theatre in October 1963, on the invitation of Laurence Olivier who was then at the helm of the theatre. It is said Tynan opted for the term literary manager as the board believed the term dramaturge sounded too German for post-war sensibilities. Tynan's remit at the National Theatre included programming important new works and developing new writing. He was a highly respected theatre commentator, noted particularly for his early recognition of the importance to British Theatre of John Osborne's *Look Back in Anger* (1956) when it premiered at the Royal Court during the English Stage Company's first season at the Sloane Square venue in London.[17] As such, Tynan was perceived to have his finger on the pulse of theatre, and broader cultural trends. Throughout his decade in the post at the National Theatre, Tynan challenged traditional management structures and by doing so, indirectly shaped the job of literary manager on these islands, evolving his position into a job that now differs somewhat from that of the continental dramaturge, even if the specifics of the position vary from theatre to theatre.

In due course, other institutions followed the National Theatre's lead. The Royal Court, where the angry-young-men and kitchen-sink movement had emerged in the late 1950s and early 1960s, appointed Harriet Devine[18] as their first literary manager in 1967. She had trained as an actor initially, and recalls the informal early days of the position at the Court. Devine later became an academic, author, and book reviewer. In her interview with me for this guidebook, she reflects on her time as the Court's first literary manager:

Figure 1.6 Harriet Devine, the First Literary Manager at The Royal Court Theatre, 1968.

SH: *Sue Healy*

HD: *Harriet Devine*

SH: What title were you given when you took up the position?

HD: I was the Literary Manager at the Royal Court Theatre.

SH: You trained as an actor, so how did you come to be in the literary manager role?

HD: I'd been around the Court for some years, involved in the young writers' programme. In 1966, I was approached by the new artistic director Bill Gaskill,[19] asking if I would be his assistant. My father[20] had died earlier that year, and it would never have happened if he'd been alive. He was so against nepotism. Bill and I hit it off really well and I helped him particularly in terms of script reading and selection. After about nine months or so, he asked if I could keep an eye on the whole thing and made me literary manager. I was around 23 at the time and had graduated from drama school, but I had a small child and it was a position I could fit around motherhood.

SH: How would you describe the Court's literary department at that time?

HD: It was very ad hoc; there was little organisation. Scripts were handed out to be read to whoever was at hand, there was no system really. As literary manager, I was given a corner in someone else's office and I came in several days a week. I remember lots of bits of paper, scripts piled up on the floor. It was all a bit chaotic. I really saw a difference when visiting Graham [Whybrow][21] in his literary manager's office decades later. The Court's literary department had changed beyond all recognition. Not only did Graham have his own office, he even had an assistant. And I was particularly struck by how the focus was very much on working with the playwright by then.

SH: **Were you heading a reading team?**

HD: We tended to ask those around the Court to read scripts. I remember Keith Johnstone was one of the readers, and the assistant directors Rob Kidd and Barry Hanson. They'd weed out the good scripts, pass them to me and I'd give a more thorough consideration and decide if I'd recommend to Bill or not.

SH: **Were readers paid?**

HD: They were paid ten shillings a script, which might get you lunch in a local café.

SH: **Did you have any other responsibilities?**

HD: I had to write a lot of rejection letters, which was my least favourite part of the job. I did arrange to meet a couple of playwrights of promise and encouraged them over the year. We didn't have any script meetings then. If I thought a script had merit and potential I passed to Bill, who made the final decision. I didn't find anyone or any script who was particularly amazing at that time. I left after a year.

SH: **Who took over from you?**

HD: Christopher Hampton.[22] He was very young, perhaps 20 or 21. Then David Hare took over from him.[23,24] Later, Donald Howarth was literary manager in the mid-1970s and I recall Donald was very keen to get black writers on.[25]

SH: **Did you enjoy the role?**

HD: I'm glad to have done it, to have had the opportunity. I was young and confident and had no doubts about my ability to assess scripts then. I don't think I would have been so ready to take the position later in life.

After Devine left, the Royal Court retained the position, and playwrights such as Hampton, Hare, Ann Jellicoe, and Howarth served as literary managers at that theatre throughout the 1970s. It was 1981, however, before the Royal Shakespeare Company installed Colin Chambers in the position at that company. By the 1990s, a growing number of theatres around England were employing a literary manager in both a full-time and part-time basis. At the point of writing, most theatres dealing with new writing will have a literary manager, although they may not be labelled as such, and confusion over the specific remit of the position remains. In Mair's view, the ambiguity is rooted in the fact that the term literary manager has been used in the past to describe entirely different jobs:

> [The term literary manager] has meant different things at different times. John Hewitt[26] was described as the literary manager at the Lyric in previous years, but that really referred to the fact that he edited a poetry magazine, a very successful one where Seamus Heaney and Michael Longley were first published – he wasn't really a theatre's literary manager in the sense we understand today. The Lyric had had artistic residencies involved some reading requirements, but there was no real template for my position. There was no set procedure or policy so yes, I often have to clarify what I do.[27]

Kostick, also working on the island of Ireland, and based in Dublin, considers why he has always had the title literary manager:

> I took [the position of literary manager at Fishamble] in 1996. In fact, I was reluctant to accept the title 'manager' at first because I had a left wing aversion to the label 'management'. To be honest, I don't think we'd heard the term 'dramaturge' at that point, I don't think it was in the lexicon so it wasn't even considered as a title for my role back then. Perhaps we were suspicious of 18th century German ideas about how good plays are constructed, I'm not sure. The first time I heard the term dramaturge was in reference to Hannah Slattne's work in Belfast.[28]

NOTES

1. Sue Healy's interview the Rebecca Mairs, via Zoom, August 10, 2021.
2. Sue Healy's interview with Fleur Hebditch, via Zoom, July 22, 2021.
3. Sue Healy's interview with Chris Campbell, London, July 21 2021
4. Sue Healy's interview with Gavin Kostick, via Zoom, July 22, 2021.
5. Sue Healy's interview with Gavin Kostick, via Zoom, July 22, 2021.
6. Sue Healy's interview with Simon Stephens, London, August 13, 2021.
7. Interview with Chris Campbell, London, July 21, 2021.
8. Interview with Fleur Hebditch, via Zoom, July 22, 2021.
9. Sue Healy's interview with Rebecca Mairs, via Zoom, August 10, 2021.
10. Fishamble's literary manager Gavin Kostick lectures in dramaturgy on this MFA at the Lír Academy. The course is also headed by Graham Whybrow who served as literary manager at the Royal Court during the theatre's notably successful 1995–2007 period.
11. Interview with Chris Campbell, London, July 21, 2021.

12 The topic of pay and the ethics of relying on volunteerism will be examined in more depth in Chapter 7 of this book.
13 Sue Healy's interview with Chris Campbell, July 21, 2021.
14 Sue Healy's interview with Gavin Kostick, July 22, 2021.
15 Sue Healy's interview with Simon Stephens, London, August 13, 2021.
16 *Dramaturgy and Performance* by Cathy Turner and Synne Behrndt.
17 Kenneth Tynan was one of only two critics who could see how, upon its premiere at the Royal Court on May 8th, 1956 the then-controversial Osborne play *Look Back in Anger,* exploded the glibly codified fairytale world of the country house play.
18 Harriet Devine interviewed at her home in France, by Sue Healy via Zoom, July 23, 2021.
19 William (Bill) Gaskill (1930–2016) was a theatre director, and artistic director at the Court 1966–1972. In 1974 he co-founded Joint Stock Theatre Company with Max Stafford-Clark, David Hare and David Aukin.
20 Harriet Devine's father was the towering mid-century theatre figure, the director and actor George Devine. He was a founding member and artistic director of the English Stage Company which established residency at the Royal Court Theatre, Sloane Square, in 1956, and remains *in situ* at the theatre today. One of their very first productions was the world premiere of John Osborne's *Look Back in Anger* (1956), a seminal text credited with a central role in the modernisation of British theatre. Devine remained at the helm of the Sloane Square institution from 1956 until his premature death in January 1966. The George Devine Award for promising new playwrights is named in his honour.
21 Graham Whybrow, a trained barrister and former visual arts books publisher, served as literary manager at the Royal Court 1994–2008. This era was a remarkable period in the Court's new writing history, with the theatre situating itself at the hub of what later became known as the in-yer-face movement, an oppositional, provoking and confrontational trend in theatre noted for its propensity to shock. Whybrow's tenure as literary manager at the Court was further characterised by his advocating for and championing of emerging talents of note, including Sarah Kane, Martin McDonagh, Lucy Prebble, Jez Butterworth and Simon Stephens.
22 Christopher Hampton is a playwright, screenwriter and film director. He served as literary manager at the Royal Court Theatre 1968–1970.
23 David Hare is a playwright, screenwriter, theatre and film director. He was invited to become resident dramatist at the Court in 1970, by Hampton with whom he'd earlier attended the independent school, Lancing.
24 A note on gatekeeping: upon Hare's departure in 1972, the new artistic director Oscar Lewenstein was keen make the Court less of a middle-class, white, male and English boys' club. Lewenstein appointed the female playwrights Ann Jellicoe as literary manager and Caryl Churchill as resident dramatist. The former's responsibilities incorporated more administrative responsibilities, the latter's were more dramaturgical – though there was overlap. Lewenstein was also determined to provide space for native Irish work, which had hitherto been neglected lamentably by the Court. Immediately upon assuming his artistic directorship in the autumn of 1972, Lewenstein programmed the Irish voice: *Richard's Cork Leg* (1962) by Brendan Behan and *A Pagan Place* (1972) by Edna O'Brien were both shown on the main stage that first Lewenstein season,

and *Eye Winker, Tom Tinker* (1972) by Tom Mac Intyre which was produced in the Theatre Upstairs. The following year, Lewenstein gave platform to a comment on the Troubles, *Freedom of the City* (1973) by Derry writer Brian Friel, which went on the main stage (much to the chagrin of the old guard and the Arts Council). Lewenstein further appointed the Irish playwright Wilson John Haire as resident dramatist in 1974. This advocacy helped to provide native Irish theatre with validation and attention that it had not previously enjoyed to any great degree beyond the island of Ireland.

25 Donald Howarth (1931–2020) was a playwright and theatre director. In 1975, he was invited to become literary manager at the Court on the invitation of the producer and artistic director at that time, Oscar Lewenstein. Howarth stayed in this role for over a year. Having lived in South Africa where he was active in anti-apartheid theatre, Howarth was a champion of black writing and black performers. As he explained in a 2018 interview with me:

> I'd been working in South Africa and I had come back home and found it was not much different. I said we had our own version of apartheid here, that there were no black members on the [Court's] Artistic Committee and us whites made all the decisions. I said I would like to mix things up a bit.

During Howarth's tenure as literary manager, writers from the global majority were given a more visible platform at the Court. – Interview with Sue Healy, 9 Lower Mall, 2018.

26 John Hewitt (1951–2008), Northern Irish actor and one time artistic director at the Lyric Theatre, Belfast.
27 Sue Healy's interview with Rebecca Mairs, via Zoom, August 10, 2021.
28 Sue Healy's interview with Gavin Kostick, via Zoom, July 22, 2021.

CHAPTER 2

Attracting unsolicited scripts

Evaluating new writing is an incredibly rewarding and interesting if time-consuming aspect of the literary manager's work. Setting up an efficient system for attracting and processing unsolicited material should be top of your to-do list. New writing submitted to theatres for consideration will fall into two categories: **unsolicited** scripts and **solicited** scripts. Unsolicited scripts refer to the work sent into your theatre without a specific invitation. These submissions from the general public will comprise the majority of scripts your theatre receives. More often than not, unsolicited scripts are by early career playwrights not yet represented by an agent, and some without any experience of writing at all. A great many will not show any promise, but there are always some diamonds in the rough – and finding one is what it is all about, that is where the thrill of literary management lies.

Encouraging a wide selection of work allows you and your reading team to more easily spot new trends emerging in writing, to observe what topics are currently capturing the imaginations of writers, to determine what influences are holding fast, and to single out innovative writing. In short, an unsolicited script pile enables the literary manager to take the temperature of the nation.

Unsolicited scripts also give you and your reading team an opportunity to hone and improve your dramaturgical skills. As time-consuming as sifting through and measuring the value of unsolicited work can be, these scripts are the lifeblood of a literary department and if your theatre deals in new writing, unsolicited scripts are fundamental to a healthy literary department.

Figure 2.1 A script-filled room at 9 Lower Mall, London, Former Home of George Devine Co-founder of The English Stage Company at the Royal Court Theatre, and later of playwright and literary manager Donald Howarth.

ENCOURAGING THE RECEIPT OF UNSOLICITED SCRIPTS

Give thought to having a submissions tab on your theatre's website, a specific destination for script submissions. Once you've set this up, contact established websites and publications broadly read by playwrights and ask them to help you promote any submissions opportunity you might launch. Social media is also your friend here, post and share as much as you can and encourage your readers, followers, and friends of the theatre to follow suit. Below are some suggested places you can advertise for unsolicited scripts.

BBC Writersroom
London Playwrights Blog
The Stage
Theatre.ie

As fascinating and rewarding as unsolicited scripts potentially are, evaluating them takes up a lot of time and you will have to consider ways to efficiently manage this process. To provide an example of volume, the Finborough Theatre, a small, 50-seat fringe venue in London, receives approximately 1,000 unsolicited scripts per year. Even Fishamble, a non-venue company in Ireland receives over 260 scripts annually.[1] Bigger venues including the Royal Court or the National Theatre will get many times that figure. Depending on your reading resources, you might consider limiting your acceptance of unsolicited scripts to a defined period. Perhaps ring-fence a six-week submission window every year and advertise on your website when this occurs. Serious writers with a particular interest in your theatre will take note and will send in work when the submission window rolls around. Retain the submissions page for the balance of the year, but disable submissions outside the window period. Use the page instead to let writers know the type of plays your theatre is interested in reading, and what you're definitely not keen on. It might be a good idea to have a list of answers to FAQs.

You'd be well advised to have a dedicated email account for receiving unsolicited submissions. It's a tidier approach that will help with your filing. Moreover, keeping submission emails separate from day-to-day administration correspondence will further guard against scripts going AWOL. Such an email account also quickly reveals how many submissions you are receiving, which in turn makes the process easier to manage.

ADVISING WRITERS ON WHAT TO SUBMIT

In order to save time and confusion all-round, your submissions page should clearly state the following information:

A) If you have a 'submission window' or if receipt is ongoing/rolling.

B) If your theatre is looking for a particular type of play.

C) The required presentation and format, and the process and route of submission.

D) A brief overview of what will happen to the script upon receipt.

E) What the writer can expect as a result of this process.

F) How long a response might take.

Figure 2.2 Scripts at 9 Lower Mall, Former Home of George Devine Co-Founder of The English Stage Company at The Royal Court Theatre, and later of playwright and literary manager Donald Howarth.

Although such a list might seem quite prescriptive, I recommend you are as explicit as possible on the above. The succinct and prominent provision of this information on your website will save time and confusion all round.

Don't assume any knowledge. State that you are specifically looking for stage plays, otherwise you'll receive a fair share of screenplays, novels, short stories, and the like. Perhaps include a FAQs list where you can anticipate and answer common queries such as "what is the length of a full-length play?" (that one is always difficult to answer with precision, though a rule-of-thumb might be "no shorter than 45-pages").

Occasionally, an enthusiastic writer might submit a number of their plays at once. It's best to discourage multiple submissions from a single writer, however, in order to more fairly distribute time allocated to all playwrights. If you are receiving a great number of submissions, it may be an idea to limit acceptance to a single submission per writer per 12-month period. Of course, if you find a writer with a particularly striking voice, you can always request more work immediately and directly, but it is best not to make that an open policy. Refining in this way will also help you obtain a more even and broad view of the new writing terrain; it's ultimately fairer.

Ensure playwrights know precisely the type of work your theatre is seeking. If yours is a theatre known for, say, biting political work or historical dramas or comedy, mention this fact prominently on your submissions page. Likewise, if you know you'll never programme a musical, or a monologue, state this fact in a plain and uncomplicated way. You'll still receive some, but they'll be fewer. Don't assume that everyone submitting will be familiar with your theatre's leanings as many playwrights will be

Figure 2.3 Criterion New Writing Program, Financed by the Criterion Theatre Trust.

submitting from far away, other countries even. Unambiguous and precise direction at this stage helps everyone and can save you time and resources, and the writer disappointment, down the line. It is, of course, a good idea to suggest that any writers interested in sending work to your theatre might visit the venue and familiarise themselves with the work regularly programmed there, if at all possible (and it often isn't).

If you will not be providing feedback, be plain on this point before they submit. State how you will and won't receive copy – some theatres won't accept a link to a hosted script on another website, for example. Do you only accept hard copy? Or only electronic copies? It's unusual these days for a theatre not to accept electronic copies of course, but a dwindling number still prefer paper over screen. It is worth being mindful of printing costs, and the related postal costs, can be expensive and new writers who are often young, don't have pots of disposable income. I remember when I was an MA student, one theatre requested I send them two hard copies of my latest play if I wanted them to consider it. It cost me half my food budget for the week to print off and mail these scripts to them (to another country) – and they never had the decency to respond, at all. Such thoughtless actions can infuriate an impoverished (and hangry) student. Be considerate.

Having a submission window is advisable, as you can allocate quieter months for reading. You may decide, however, not to advertise that you will accept unsolicited scripts, and only agree to read scripts recommended to you. It will depend on your own situation, your set strategies, and how you plan to progress as an institution. The key is to always be direct and unclouded with the writers – and avoid wasting anyone's time.

ADVISING WRITERS ON HOW TO SUBMIT

When detailing your submission procedure, instruct the playwright to supply contact details with their work, and let them know where this should appear (on the script and/or body of email, etc.). It might also be an idea to request a brief overview of the script, but always be sure to give a word or page limit on any requested synopsis. I would also suggest you give thought to file size limits, as you will likely get some submissions that include images or music – you don't want to jam up your inbox. I have found that requesting a writer's bio is also frequently useful, as it will reveal what influences and experiences have shaped their writing. Some readers prefer anonymous scripts however.

Decide if you want a hard copy or electronic copy of scripts. For reasons of ease, cost and the saving of trees, electronic submission is by far the most common method today, but if you insist on hard copies make this very explicit (and possibly explain why). If you prefer to be emailed scripts, explain how you'd like them formatted. State if you have a leaning for *PDF*s, or if *Microsoft Word* is preferred over *Pages* or *FinalDraft*, for example. Be clear if you don't accept links to work hosted elsewhere – or state if you do.

Don't be afraid to suggest type-faces and font sizes or other industry-standard approaches which may be preferred by your reading team. For the new playwright,

Figure 2.4 Criterion New Writing Program, Financed by the Criterion Theatre Trust.

this instruction provides them with the best chance for their work to be viewed as professional. It may be helpful to include a page of sample script layout on your website, as in the illustration here. If you post a real extract by a contemporary playwright, ensure you obtain the writer's permission in the first instance, or the permission of their estate if deceased but the work is still in copyright. This template will help new writers familiarise themselves with industry-standard layout. Remember that new writing often comes from those who are taking their first steps in their writing career and are not necessarily familiar with such details, so don't worry, you are helping and not patronising. More pertinently, having scripts in a similar format levels the playing field, ensuring fairness all round. The following is an example of the type of sample you could supply:

The Noble Gate

A play by Jane-Clare Bard
Jane-Clare Bard
Vicar's Rest
Watlington
Oxford OX49 9AD
UK
07971 173156
JCBard@yahoo.co.uk

Characters

Meghan Turner 20s. Norfolk accent.
Keith Andrews Late 50s. Londoner.

Setting

Meghan's council flat studio, Norwich city centre, April 2022.

A Note on the text

The following marks denote the following intentions
A succession of dots (…) indicates a hesitation.
A hyphen (–) indicates a break in speech.
A forward slash (/) indicates the character that speaks next should begin with their line, overlapping with the preceding character's dialogue.

Scene one

Meghan's council flat/studio, Norwich city centre, 2022. Lights up on a small living space/bedroom. It's unkempt, looks stuffy and unaired. Posters on the walls show complex mathematical theorems. It is night.

> MEGHAN *is in bed, scrolling on her phone, it's entertaining her, she's lost in that world. Suddenly, she stops, thinks she hears something outside and gets up, darts over to the window to peer through the curtains. Nothing. She returns to bed and her phone, loses herself once more. A loud KNOCK on the door. Meghan drops her phone.*
>
> **KEITH** (*Off*) Babe?
>
> **MEGHAN** Keith?
>
> **KEITH** (*Off*) Yeah.
>
> > /BEAT/
>
> **MEGHAN** Come in.
>
> **KEITH** (*Off*) The door won't open on its own.
>
> > *Meghan doesn't move for a few moments.*
>
> **MEGHAN** Won't open?
>
> **KEITH** (*Off*) I don't have a key.
>
> **MEGHAN** I'll get mine.
>
> > *Meghan goes to the door. Here hand hovers over the door key in the latch.*
>
> **KEITH** (Off. *Laughing*). If you want me to /
>
> **MEGHAN** /I'm trying to find my key, I said.
>
> > *Meghan takes he key from the door, throws it onto the bed. Keith knocks.*
>
> **MEGHAN** I'm looking for it.

You could always post a sample in *Lorem Ipsum*, which will ensure readers focus on format rather than the readable content (as often, new writers will try to imitate the style and tone of a sample on your website, which is not what the literary manager wants).

> Example of *Lorem Ipsum* script:
>
> **The Noble Gate**
>
> by Jane-Clare Bard
> Jane-Clare Bard
> Vicar's Rest
> Watlington
> Oxford OX49 9AD
> UK
> 07971 173156
> JCBard@yahoo.co.uk

Characters

Meghan Turner 20s. Norfolk accent.
Keith Andrews Late 30s. Londoner.

Setting

Meghan's council flat/studio, Norwich city centre, April 2022.

A Note on the text

The following marks denote the following intentions
A succession of dots (…) indicates a hesitation.
A hyphen (–) indicates a break in speech.
A forward slash (/) indicates the character that speaks next should begin with their line, overlapping with the preceding character's dialogue.

Scene one

MEGHAN *gratiam ille, Supremi typi exequi, 2022. Patria ea ad a animi hilari eorum/decursu. Te et se vestram earum, fusce tutori nam saevire. Disordo ea est minim eros medicus criminalibus princeps.*

Mi et dicta.

E sunt error ea est quas. Gradum donec per harum.

KEITH (*Off*) Modo?

MEGHAN Keith?

KEITH (*Off*) Quae. Hac consortio adverso quis!

MEGHAN Quos si.

KEITH (*Off*) Modo. V non'w arcu a sed/

    Meghan doesn't move for a few moments.

MEGHAN /Quo'm quod?

KEITH (*Off*) Te vacare. O'ti iste aut erat.

MEGHAN Perare louor ab hac nibh hic cras.

    Meghan's goes to the door. Her hand hovers over the door key in the latch.

KEITH (Off. *Laughing*). Custos li orci est non/

MEGHAN /Hac consortio adverso quis? M'ii typi il et w certum!

    Meghan takes the key from the door, throws it onto the bed. Keith knocks.

MEGHAN Perare louor ab hac… Nibh hic cras, custos li orci est non.

INFORMING THE WRITER OF WHAT HAPPENS NEXT

As many writers submitting unsolicited material are novices, this submission will be their first encounter with a literary department. They won't be familiar with the reading procedure and time frames. Understandably, new writers are often excited and sometimes impatient for news of how their first script is faring, and are keen to know if it has impressed. Expect to receive emails in chase of news, sometimes days after receipt of the script. In order to manage expectations, therefore, you might want to detail the likely journey of a script on your submissions page and provide an approximate time frame from receipt to reply. An illustrated timeline of the process should be reader-friendly and very clear and uncomplicated.

A sample explaining your process might look like the following:

> Within **two weeks** of receipt: Your submission is received and logged by the literary department.
>
> Within **six weeks** of receipt: The theatre sends your work to a general reader who gives your script an initial read. They decide if it is a play is one that might interest us. If the reader decides this is not a work we would take further, you should hear from the literary department within this time frame. Please remember that if your work is turned down at this point, don't be disheartened it may very well find a home elsewhere. Have a fresh look at the text, tweak if you wish, and send it on to another theatre.
>
> Within **ten weeks** of receipt: If the theatre feels your script should be given another, closer read, we will send your work to a senior reader or the literary manager, who will make a decision on further action. Even if you don't make it past this point, it is likely you'll be encouraged to send more work as there is some aspect of your writing that clearly appeals. You are now on our radar.
>
> Within **three months** of receipt: Should your work pique the interest of the literary manager and/or artistic director, you or your agent will be contacted to set up a meeting. It is most likely that the literary manager will simply want to meet you and get to know you, as they find you interesting as a playwright and would like to see how we might support your development. Please be aware that a meeting is rarely an indication that your work is about to be programmed. Often at this point, the literary manager will want to invite you to join our (in-house writer development scheme/young or community writers' group or some similar new writing initiative, or perhaps discuss a rehearsed reading of your work).

Of course, the above are merely examples. The time frames and processes will differ depending on the size of the theatre, the literary department, and the time demands on the literary manager – but the above is an indication of what is normal, reasonable, and acceptable. In his interview for this guide, the playwright Simon Stephens, who has worked closely with the leading new writing theatres in the country, admits that the wait can be trying, but is generous in his understanding of the situation:

> A literary manager can be overwhelmed by administration. It's different in TV production, they have more resources and there's a much quicker turnaround on scripts. I recently wrote two TV pilots and was startled to receive feedback within 24 hours. That wouldn't happen in theatre and waiting can be very difficult for a writer. Writing is exposing work and delays in response can make even the most experienced writers feel paranoid. It can be difficult for writers to have to wait as long as they do to get an answer from a literary manager, but it is because literary departments are often slightly funded and have so much admin to do.[2]

In my experience as literary manager, and also on the other side of the fence as a playwright, when this system breaks down is usually at the last hurdle. That is to say, if a play is recommended up the chain until it's at the door of the literary manager or the artistic director – it's then that it can get waylaid or neglected, as these two busy figures can have their attention snagged by a more demanding issue. Try to ensure that no matter what, every playwright receives a response and that there is a logging system in place to check this happens. If your website states that all playwrights will have a response within, say, three months, then make sure that happens and if a playwright contacts to say they've been waiting longer than this – chase up the play as quickly as you can, and apologise for that delay.

The length of time will, of course, greatly depend on the size of your reading team and what resources you have. It is standard for a writer to expect a waiting period of six weeks to three months, particularly for an unsolicited script. Explaining the steps on your submissions page will help them to feel connected to the process – and to be patient when they don't hear back from you immediately. Ensure you outline how the script will initially be read by the reading team and assessed, and if of interest to the theatre, it will be passed up the pyramid to the artistic team for a closer read. Let writers know at what point in the process they should expect to hear from the theatre. And always make sure that the writers receive some sort of reply, if you state that you provide replies.

The literary manager hopes that the unsolicited pile will churn up a writer of promise. If this happens, they will build a relationship between the playwright and the theatre in the hope that a script of strong quality will emerge at a later point. You'll do well to remember that every single well-known playwright today, from Phoebe Waller-Bridge and Michaela Coel to James Graham and Martin McDonagh, has had their work in a theatre's unsolicited pile at some point, and it took a keen

Figure 2.5 Bush Theatre, Shepherd's Bush.

eye to single them out, and a skilled literary manager to nurture and champion their talent. Your job as literary manager is not to find the perfect play, but to recognise potential. A unique voice should be encouraged and fostered to the point where it can produce a strong play.

The unsolicited pile can reveal the *zeitgeist*. It is a fascinating to see, suddenly, very similar plays arriving via this route. Sometimes writers are evidently being directly influenced by trends and fashions in writing. Sometimes it's a general malaise in times of strife, other trends are perhaps due to an influence coming from a popular TV show. Following the success of Phoebe Waller-Bridge's stage-play *Fleabag* (2013) and the much-lauded TV adaptation (2016), literary departments across the country witnessed a tsunami of single female monologues featuring a sexually liberated but angry young woman with a penchant for breaking the fourth wall. Sometimes, however, it's harder to pinpoint the root of the trend. For a couple of years before the travails of Brexit and Trump – a great number of plays received were of the near-future dystopia ilk, as if writers could sense the unease and turmoil down the line. At the time of writing, as we've recently emerged from COVID19 lockdown, only witness the Russian invasion and ensuing war break out in Ukraine, the unsolicited piles are showing a leaning towards the supernatural, and particularly plays exploring time travel. What this means, only time will tell, but it is fascinating.

NOTES

1   Sue Healy's interview with Gavin Kostick, via Zoom, July 22, 2021.
2   Sue Healy's interview with Simon Stephens, London, August 13, 2021.

CHAPTER 3

Systems, structures, and approaches

THE DAY-TO-DAY OPERATIONS OF A LITERARY DEPARTMENT

As the position of literary manager is quite varied in terms of responsibilities, no two literary departments function in the same way or operate an identical schedule. Depicting a literary manager's quotidian procedure is a challenge. There are a number of commonalities, however. Fleur Hebditch describes her department's practice at the Stephen Joseph Theatre in Scarborough:

> I come in in the mornings and look at the excel sheet for the plays we've received in our submission window and I'll do whatever admin might need doing on that. This will often involve triaging the work, sending out to first volunteer readers with a synopsis and asking for their thoughts on the initial pages. If it merits it, we'll then give a play a full read and provide a fuller analysis. If recommended after that, it's back for another full read and we'll decide what we might do with it. I may be on the look-out for a particular type of play, perhaps a farce for example. Normally, if we are happy with it, I'll send it to the artistic director at this point and perhaps suggest a public play reading. We might offer a seed commission, which is £1,000. Unfortunately, only a very few texts will get to this stage. I have to send a lot of rejection letters to a lot of writers which is the hardest part of the job. I am very aware of how much time and creativity goes into each play. Rejection letters are never easy to send. I always make sure I don't send them out on a Friday evening. You don't want people going into their weekend in disappointment.

> When the literary work is done, I put on my production hat and I get involved with the programming, casting etc. It's pretty collaborative.
>
> We have a Christmas show every year, and I'll give notes on that. We have a studio where most of the new writing goes. I love new writing but it doesn't get as much attention as the main work – unless it's Alan Ayckbourn's.[1]

Similarly, at the Lyric in Belfast, literary manager Rebecca Mairs outlines a week in her literary department:

> There is no such thing as a typical week, but I will have about eight to 12 meetings with writers per week, often on the back of an initiative we're running. I also need to be available to read work. On average, I have about ten projects on our slate. I try to concentrate the reading of new scripts into six-eight weeks. I have to read everything that comes in in the specified windows, and analyse it and respond to it.[2]

It is particularly instructive to learn of a playwright's experience of a literary department, and the highs and lows of their interaction with the literary manager. Simon Stephens has been complimentary and quick to give credit to all the literary managers and dramaturges who have supported his career from its beginning to his present position as one of the most established playwrights in Britain. Here, he outlines his journey from his first meeting with a theatre's dramaturge to a call from the Royal Court's literary manager, which resulted in the production of his first play:

> The first play I ever had performed was *Bluebird*, but it was actually my eighth play. I'd written seven plays previously when I was at university in York. I moved to Edinburgh shortly afterwards and sent some of my work to what was then The New Traverse Theatre. I was contacted by Ella Wildridge who introduced herself as a dramaturge with the theatre and invited me in for a cup of coffee. It was in the mid-1990s, I was 23.
>
> This meeting was significant because she was an industry figure encouraging me and this instills confidence. At last, here I had someone who telling me that my writing was interesting and had value, and that encouragement was invaluable.
>
> I left Edinburgh shortly afterwards, which was silly in a way as there was so much happening there at the time. David Grieg and Zinnie Harris were coming to the fore, it was an exciting time.

I moved to London. In 1997 I wrote *Bluebird*. I sent it into the Royal Court Theatre who had recently appointed Ian Rickson as artistic director. At the time I was training to be a schoolteacher and was rushing to complete my dissertation. The phone rang and a voice said, "Is this Simon Stephens? I'm Graham Whybrow, Literary Manager at the Royal Court and we've read your play and we think it's wonderful." Graham asked me to meet him. I was 27. I had been trying to write plays for six years. This felt like a breakthrough.[3]

Figure 3.1 The Royal Court Theatre, Sloane Square, London.

READING AND ASSESSING UNSOLICITED SCRIPTS

It's unlikely that a lone literary manager will be able to read all submissions, unless in a tiny theatre with a very limited submissions policy – and even then it would be a challenge. As this guidebook demonstrates, a literary manager has many responsibilities and can only commit a certain amount of time to reading unsolicited scripts. As soon as you can, you'll need to set up a reading team, if one is not already in existence.

Your readers ought to be people with literary or theatre industry experience and preferably both. Experienced actors, directors, English Literature graduates, dramaturges, and other playwrights are often approached by theatres to read unsolicited material. Obviously, as the initial readers of scripts sent to your theatre, they are performing an important role. As literary manager, you must be confident your readers are equipped to make that first yes/no/maybe decision on scripts. Readers should know and understand your theatre's leanings. The most common way to ensure this is the case is to give any potential reader a test based on your theatre's preferences. This test will probably involve providing the candidate with a number of scripts your literary department has already assessed and asking the potential reader for a short report on each. Ideally, you'll present them with a script that you like very much, one you don't like at all, and one that sits in the middle. It's a simple test, but it is used widely and provides a good indication as to whether or not the reader is on the same page artistically, as your theatre.

COMMON APPROACHES AND PROCEDURES

Be vigilant in keeping a log of all unsolicited scripts received. An excel sheet is probably best for this purpose. Either this task is carried out by the literary manager or a literary department associate. You may want to set up an auto-reply on the submissions email, outlining what will happen with the script once received. As detailed in the suggested advertised website timeframe, upon receipt, a script is immediately allocated to a reader who will be instructed to give a yes/no/maybe assessment within a couple of weeks.

SCRIPTS THAT RECEIVE A 'NO'

Some 80%–90% of the unsolicited scripts you receive will not pass the first read through. Occasionally, it will be obvious even by the first few pages that the script is not one to which your reader should devote time. This can be for a variety of reasons, perhaps the playwright has plainly not read your submissions policy. It may also be that the playwright has not yet grasped the very fundamentals of dramatic writing, which makes their work difficult to read and assess. If this is the case, readers won't need to read the entire script, they can speed read, and it can be logged as an

Figure 3.2 The Finborough Theatre, West Brompton, London.

immediate 'no.' Otherwise, you should encourage your readers to read through all scripts. If, once completed, the assessment is still a 'no' you could request that the reader provides a line or two of encouraging and constructive critical feedback which you can send on to the writer. Give thought to directing your readers in the 'sandwich' approach to criticism. Always supply something positive to say, being mindful that many writers will find a rejection a crushing experience and you should encourage where you can. The response is best coming from the literary department and not the reader directly – in fact, try to keep the reader anonymous. Do bear in mind that feedback for rejected unsolicited scripts is not necessary from an unfunded theatre as it requires time resources to provide the same. Nonetheless, feedback is helpful and usually appreciated so if you can provide, do so. As a 'no' response will inevitably disappoint, I try not to send them out on a Friday afternoon, or before a holiday.

From time to time, a playwright will refuse to take 'no' for an answer. Some will offer to make suggested changes and re-submit the work to you. If a script is a straight 'no,' it's unlikely that some tweaks will change your mind. Moreover, you probably don't want to spend your time re-reading scripts you've already considered, albeit in modified form. I have found that a good, if imperfect, solution is a policy not to reconsider scripts assessed as 'no.' Wish the playwright well and politely decline, telling them you'd be interested in seeing their next play in a year's time. It's also advisable to direct the playwright to other theatres receiving unsolicited scripts, and supply links to these websites if possible. It may simply be that this playwright's work doesn't suit your theatre but will find an enthusiastic home elsewhere, and it is helpful to say so. Be respectful at all times and don't engage if a playwright resorts to anger and insult. Such instances are thankfully incredibly rare, but do occur. It can be difficult and upsetting when this happens but it is a testament to how personal this work is to writers. 'Polite but firm' should be your mantra. As the former literary manager at the Royal Court, Chris Campbell, helpfully advises when dealing a writer who is finding it difficult to accept a 'no':

It happens, but thankfully rarely. Firstly, you must take the heat out of the situation if things get fraught. Writing a letter is better in[4] this situation. It gives [the writer] time to digest the news – speaking is not helpful as they tend not hear anything after you say 'no' anyway. Say you'd be happy to discuss later if they'd like. Always be truthful, don't leave anything open to interpretation. You can say that the theatre cannot respond to the play, which might make it more objective. I remember reading some old archive letters from Kenneth Tynan at the National and he very succinctly would write two lines or so saying, "I can't interest anyone at the theatre in this play," – which brings in some objectivity but is also very clear. At the Court we always tried to write helpful rejection letters. In fact, I remember an American playwright who wrote to say that he held on to the rejection letters he received from British theatres as they are so charming. And it's quite a surprise when you finally realise that your play is being rejected. So, perhaps that is not such a good thing, maybe we need to be a bit more direct!

SCRIPTS THAT RECEIVE A 'MAYBE'

These are scripts that the reader thinks might have some potential, and they don't feel a 'no' is a fair reflection of the work, but aren't sure if the script is a 'yes.' Perhaps the reader is questioning if the work suits the theatre, for example. Or, maybe one aspect of the writing is quite strong, but the script is let down in other areas. These scripts, roughly comprising 8%–10% of submitted work, will be passed to a more senior reading for further, more considered, assessment. If the second reader says no but agrees that the script has merit, write an encouraging reply to the playwright, perhaps requesting to see another sample of their work as soon as they are ready to send it.

SCRIPTS THAT RECEIVE A 'YES!'

A straight 'yes' response to an unsolicited script is rare, perhaps 2% of all those submitted are labelled with the affirmative. As with the 'maybes' such a script is sent to a senior member of the reading team for a second read – which may be carried out by the literary manager. It's always exciting when a nugget of gold is churned up! If you as literary manager also react positively to the script, you will then discuss its potential with the artistic director. It's unusual for a script to go from blind submission to production however, what is more likely is that you'll meet with the writer and discuss developmental possibilities and ways to build your relationship. You might have in mind a reading of the work, or dramaturgical support, or championing the playwright in some form or other. All will depend on the writer and the script itself. Do take time to enjoy the moment however!

RESPONDING TO THE WRITER – UNSOLICITED SCRIPTS

It cannot be stressed enough how important it is to be respectful and considerate in ensuring that all playwrights receive an answer and within a reasonable timeframe. When you are dealing with a tide of scripts, it is easy to lose sight of the fact that each play represents a great amount of time and work on the part of the playwright – their hopes and dreams are invested in those 70-odd pages of script. Always make sure your spreadsheet has a check box noting whether or not the playwright has received a reply, and within the promised time frame. This approach is simply good manners, but it will also guard against bringing your venue into disrepute on social media.

A version of the following templates can be adapted to suit your venue:

Sample text for replies:

'No'

> Dear [insert name],
>
> Thank you for submitting [insert title] to [insert venue name] for consideration. We very much appreciate your interest in our theatre. Our literary team has read and assessed your script and unfortunately, we don't feel this is a work we will be taking forward on this occasion.
>
> Our reader made the following notes, which you may find helpful: [insert short feedback – positive aspect > area for improvement > encouraging close].
>
> We sincerely wish you all the best in your future writing career. We respectfully ask that writers wait a 12-month period before submitting another script to our department as we wish to ensure all playwrights receive equal attention, but we look forward to reading more of your work after that time.
>
> Very best wishes,
>
> [Venue name]

'Maybe'

When composing a response to a 'maybe' script, perhaps provide a short analysis of the plot, character, theme, and message. If possible, measure its success as a piece of theatre. Asking a question can be a useful and diplomatic way of helping a writer at this point.

Dear [insert name]

Thank you for submitting [insert title] to [insert venue name] for consideration. We appreciate your interest in our theatre. Whilst we don't feel that this script is one we can programme right now, it impressed us and reached our senior reading team who provided the following feedback which you may find helpful: [insert short feedback > positive aspect > area for improvement > encouraging close].

Although we are not inclined to programme this particular script, we believe your work shows merit and promise and we would be keen to see another script of yours. Please feel free to send on your next work when it is ready and we'll be very happy to take a look.

Very best wishes,

[Your name]

Literary Manager.

Figure 3.3

'Yes'

Emails to writers whose work has earned a 'yes' from the literary team will be more personal and will depend on which specific approach the literary manager and the artistic director decide in taking forward the work and/or their relationship with the writer. In this instance, I find a phone call works best and suggest a face-to-face meeting if possible. The following chapter examines this point in more detail.

ASSESSING AND RESPONDING TO SOLICITED SCRIPTS

Solicited scripts refer to scripts that have been actively sought by you and/or your theatre, with a view to either programming the work or developing a relationship with the playwright. These solicited scripts can arrive via a number of avenues. You or another member of the artistic team may have been made aware of a writer's work and have contacted either the playwright directly or their agent and requested a sample script. Alternatively, perhaps you've read a positive review of a production and you feel it may be a good fit for your theatre and have requested the script, or another by the same playwright, for consideration. Maybe an agent you've worked with frequently and who knows your theatre well has flagged up a script they believe would suit your programme. Likewise, it's possible that a playwright with whom your theatre has an established relationship has sent through their latest work. Put simply, they're scripts you've requested to see.

Solicited scripts are normally sent either directly to the literary manager or to the artistic director. More often than not, these scripts are by more established and experienced playwrights and will be of a reasonably high standard. For this reason, you will not put them through the first stage sift with your readers. Solicited scripts will immediately be given a thorough and considered read by a senior member of the artistic team, and most likely this will be you. You should endeavour to provide a response within a month of receipt.

All solicited scripts should receive a rigorous read and a full report. They may all be read by you, the literary manager, or by an experienced and trusted senior member of your reading team. This senior reader should be encouraged to draft their report along the lines of the 'sandwich' suggested above, highlighting both the positives and negatives, but in more depth. This report should also be candid, it's not written for the playwright to read. You might want to provide the playwright with an edited, more positive version of the feedback.

Sample report on a solicited script:

Play: *I Am Chambers*
Playwright: Ronald McCain
Contact: RonaldTMcCain76@gmail.com
Read on: 01/12/22
Reader: Seán Bohan

Synopsis

In a dystopian future, a group of migrant labourers try to expose a corrupt council's sinister migrant recruitment practices.

In the near future, during an extremely cold winter, a local council of an unnamed English coastal city has resorted to enticing migrant workers to relocate to their town to provide badly needed manual labour. The poverty-stricken workers are attracted by the promise of free food and board and good earnings. On arrival, their passports are confiscated, however, and they are essentially enslaved. Fruzsi and Miksa, a pair of such labourers, have escaped and are in hiding. They want to expose the council's doings, and to warn others from coming to the city. Mayor Chambers dispatches Agent Wilson to kill them, but Wilson's persuaded to join their cause and gains a recording that proves the local government and Chambers are involved in modern-day slavery. Miksa's family has been threatened and his wife is killed. Their recording is successfully posted to the Internet, and a revolution starts is ignited. Fruzsi exploits her past relationship with Chambers to capture him, and she and Miksa force him to record a resignation speech. Miksa and Wilson's increasingly tense relationship reaches breaking point and, during a fight, Miksa kills Wilson before Fruzsi drags him away to join her in leading the revolt.

Response

Positives

The play features a few interesting thoughts on the theme of survival, using the recurring motif of sinking boats to explain and link different characters' behaviour and actions. Some of the dialogue is well written with good tension and fine balance of power between characters, plus the scene where Miksa attempts to save his wife is touching and brings a welcome personal angle to events.

Negatives

The characters can feel a little one-dimensional and lacking in truly individual voices. The world they inhabit doesn't feel very well developed, beyond a few general features (particularly in a piece trying to deal with complex issues, it needs to be drawn in more detail). In trying to cover such a vast subject (conditions for migrant workers, and a controlling council, in tandem with a widespread uprising) the play doesn't tackle any specific idea or theme in sufficient detail, leaving it feeling vague at times. Given the very dark nature of the subject matter, at no point in the script (other than the brief scene with Miksa and his wife) do we get a strong sense of how horrific the situation is, or the danger people are in.

SOURCING SOLICITED SCRIPTS AND SPOTTING PLAYWRIGHTS OF NOTE

Listen to your readers and other contacts in the industry. If a playwright's name comes up a few times, it is worth checking the writer out. Script submission is one door in for writers, but there are other ways their work can come to your attention. Make sure you or members of your literary team are attending scratch nights, readings, self-funded productions, and plays-without-décor – where new writing talent will be on display. Be aware of new writing awards and always make sure you check the short lists and long lists. Presently, in Britain and Ireland, the main awards are, and as literary manager you should research and gather as much information on all the awards and events listed below (and give serious thought to encouraging playwrights you are mentoring to enter, if ready):

The Bruntwood Prize

The George Devine Award

The Verity Bargate Prize

The Alfred Fagon Award (for Black British playwrights)

The ETPEP

The Susan Smith Blackburn Award (for those identifying as women)

The Stewart Parker Award (Ireland/Irish)

The Channel 4 Playwrights' Scheme

The Dublin Fringe

The Edinburgh Fringe

The Oireachtas Literary Awards

P.J. O'Connor Radio Drama Award

Phelim Donlon Playwrights Bursary and Residency

Irish Times Theatre Awards

Zebbie Awards

Eamon Keane Full Length Play Award

Fishamble – A Play for Ireland

Susan Blackburn Smith Award

Your contacts are your collateral. When you join your theatre as literary manager, you'll likely be bringing to the venue your own hard-won connections with agents and playwrights and these will be very useful going forward. Do remember to also take time to research established relationships the theatre has with writers and theatre professionals, and write and introduce yourself to all. I like to meet these associates for coffee and explain precisely the type of work we're seeking going forward. A good literary manager should be on first name terms with all agents in your locale, and these agents should be fully informed of what work is most likely to interest your theatre. Your own contacts and those of the theatre will combine to form a rich network you can tap into for scripts of interest.

Another source for solicited scripts is the terrain beyond your border. A playwright who has done particularly well in the fringe theatres of Canberra, Chicago, or Cape Town might be interested in production at your theatre. Any literary manager worth their salt will be keeping a side-eye on international trends and rising names in theatre-writing worldwide. Get to know the leading review sheets and sites throughout the Anglophone world and regularly check for stand out reviews (or have a member of the literary team do so as a weekly task). If one is of interest, write to them and request the script in order to get a better sense of the writer's work. Making contact is usually achieved via a google search for the playwright's contact, or that of their agent. Should this fail to yield contact information, get in touch with the theatre that hosted the production and they should provide access to the playwright. They are usually very happy to oblige.

Work in other languages is also another potential place to search for scripts of merit. If you have a second language, this is helpful. A large NPO theatre like the

Figure 3.4 Paris Metro.

Royal Court will possibly have an international department but most will not. If you're monolingual, get to know leading translators of plays in your area. Let them know you'd be keen to consider translations of new writing, and again, make sure they are aware of the types of plays that interest you.

If you need more information about a newly translated play or find a theatre translator for a play you're considering, translator William Gregory, who translates from Spanish to English and have worked extensively with the Royal Court, suggests exploring the following sites on file:

> The Translators Association (part of the Society of Authors) https://societyofauthors.org/Groups/Translators
> The British Centre for Literary Translation (part of UEA) https://www.uea.ac.uk/groups-and-centres/british-centre-for-literary-translation
> The Emerging Translators Network https://emergingtranslatorsnetwork.wordpress.com/
> TinT, the Theatre in Translation Network (US-based but has plenty of UK-based members) https://tintnet.org/index.html
> Performing International Plays (a research project, has specific plays associated it, rather than being an association or directory) https://www.performinginternationalplays.com/

AGENTS

One of the first actions a literary manager will take when they start in a new position is to let the industry know they've arrived. The form and reach of this announcement will depend on the size and status of your theatre. If yours is a venue of international import, if you've been made literary manager at the Royal Court Theatre or The Abbey, for example, then a press release will likely be sent to a theatre-focused publication such as *The Stage*, and/or relevant talent management agencies. In rapid succession, a slew of agents will contact you vying for your time and attention, in order to set out their various stalls. If your venue is smaller, or not based in the capital city, you'll be the one contacting agents to let them know you're interested in new writing and would like to know what writing is out there.

You should be on first name acquaintanceship with all key agents. Get to know who represents whom. Learn about their leanings – and make sure you make particular time for agents whose tastes chime with you and your theatre. If possible at all, have a coffee with those agents you feel are operating within the same literary arena as you. And where this is not possible, set up a Zoom. Make sure these agents are on your mailing lists and are invited to all your theatre's events. It's important that they come to understand what you are attempting to achieve. As well as representing the best interests of their own clients, agents act as a filter for theatres in terms of passing on scripts.

The following directory is my own reference for some of the main theatre agents currently representing emerging and established playwrights across Britain and Ireland.

I include this list as an introductory sample only, and in no way present it as an exhaustive compilation of theatre talent representatives. I'm providing it here to help you start your own research into the who's who of talent management. There are other good talent agencies, and there are other equally good theatre agents working within the agencies listed here. Absence from this sample list is not intended as any comment on any agent or agency.

Also, be mindful that, though current in 2022, this list will soon date. Agents will move agencies, or shift their focus, or retire, and young guns will emerge. So, see the following chart as a base reference, one that you can update, expand, annotate and keep current.

Agency	Website	Theatre Agent(s)
David Higham Associates	www.davidhigham.co.uk	Nicky Lund
The Haworth Agency	www.haworthagency.co.uk	Georgina Ruffhead
United Agents	www.unitedagents.co.uk	Rose Cobbe, Dan Usztan, Giles Smart, Christian Ogunbanjo
Knight Hall Agency	www.knighthallagency.com	Charlotte Knight, Katie Langridge
Berlin Associates	www.berlinassociates.com	Alexandra Cory, Rachel Daniels
Independent Talent	www.independenttalent.com	Ikenna Obiekwe, Alex Rusher
Curtis Brown	www.curtisbrown.co.uk	Lily Williams
The Agency	www.theagency.co.uk	Tanya Tillett, Emily Hickman, Katie Haines
Lark Management	www.larkmanagement.co.uk	Harriet Pennington Legh
Julia Tyrell Management	www.jtmanagement.co.uk	Julia Tyrell
Cassarotto	www.cassarotto.co.uk	Imogen Sarre, Mel Kenyon, Kirsten Foster
Lisa Richards	www.lisarichardscreatives.co.uk	Jasmine Daines Pilgrem
Under New Mgmt	www.undernewmgmt.com	Marnie Podos
Judy Daish Associates	www.judydaish.com	Judy Daish
Rochelle Stevens & Co	www.rochellestevens.com	Rochelle Stevens
Alan Brodie Representation	www.alanbrodie.com	Alan Brodie

NOTES

1 Interview with Fleur Hebditch, via Zoom, July 22, 2021.
2 Sue Healy's nterview with Rebecca Mairs, via Zoom, August 10, 2021.
3 Sue Healy's interview with Simon Stephens, Brick Lane, London, August 13, 2021.
4 Sue Healy's interview with Chris Campbell, Bloomsbury, London, July 21, 2021.

CHAPTER 4

Dramaturgy

A literary manager's job will almost always involve some dramaturgy, but their professional obligations are rarely limited to dramaturgy alone. The aim of this guidebook is an introduction to the broad responsibilities of literary management; therefore, dramaturgy is not the main focus. I will only provide a simple overview of the discipline here. Should you wish to dive deeper into this fascinating subject, there are a number of excellent publications examining modern-day dramaturgy, or dramaturgy as applied by playwrights when writing, or directors when directing, or considered by critics when reviewing. A literary manager would do well to acquaint themselves with these studies to further develop, broaden, and deepen their knowledge of the subject:

Dramaturgy in the Making: A User's Guide for Theatre Practitioners by Katalin Trencsényi (Bloomsbury)
The Art of Dramaturgy by Anne Cattaneo (Yale University Press)
Essential Dramaturgy: The Mindset and Skillset by Theresa Lang (Routledge)
Dramaturgy: A Revolution in Theatre by Mary Luckhurst (Cambridge University Press)
The Routledge Companion to Dramaturgy edited by Magda Romanska (Routledge)
The Director's Craft: A Handbook for the Theatre by Katie Mitchell (Routledge)

Playwriting: Structure, Character, How and What to Write by Stephen Jeffreys (NHB)

The Contemporary Political Play: Rethinking Dramaturgical Structure by Sarah Grochala (Bloomsbury Methuen)

How to Write About Theatre: A Manual for Critics, Student and Bloggers by Mark Fisher (Bloomsbury Methuen)

EF's Visit to a Small Planet: Some Questions to Ask a Play by Elinor Fuchs (Duke University Press)

Figure 4.1 Greg Mosse Explaining Structure, Criterion New Writing Program, Financed by the Criterion Theatre Trust.

A HISTORY OF DRAMATURGY

The word itself comes from the Ancient Greek compound *dramatourgos* – a maker of plays, or someone who arranges and puts order on dramatic action. Certainly, in some Latin and Slavic languages, this root word remains synonymous with the word for playwright. In English, the word tends to denote the analysis and the construction of elements of a play.[1]

In writing his philosophical treatise *Poetics,* Aristotle can be viewed as the first-ever dramaturge. In this early example of literary criticism, Aristotle considered the great tragedies that had come before, in particular Sophocles' *Oedipus Rex*. He attempted to dissect these works in order to find reliable recipe for a good drama. With *Poetics*, Aristotle provided the world with the unities of action, time, and place – and measured the importance of the elements of plot, character, diction, thought, spectacle, and song.

According to Aristotle, drama should be:

> An imitation of an action that is serious, complete, and of certain magnitude; in language embellished with each kind of artistic ornament, the several kinds being found in separate parts of the play in the form of action, not of narrative; though pity and fear effecting the proper purgation of these emotions.[2]

In the Aristotelian approach, tragedy focuses on the powerful in society and grapples with the major theme including vengeance and murder, whilst comedy will feature the lower classes. According to Aristotle, dramatic work ought to be shown rather than told. Aristotle posited that the arrangement of the dramatic scenes is the most important element of the work. In his view, a play must take place in a single setting and have a well-ordered beginning, middle, and end, an explicit crisis and climax, followed by a resolution designed to purge emotions and provide catharsis – and provide the theatre-goer with an outlet for otherwise harmful emotions. In this tradition, the dramatic framework is considered of pinnacle importance. The notion of the dramaturge as an architectural consultant for this construction continues to today.

In more modern terms, the role of the dramaturge owes much to the 18th century German in-house critic tasked with assisting a theatre in play development and offering on-hand and early criticism of a production. The dramaturge was viewed as an intellectual, an educator who provoked the playwright or director to consider elements of a work in a fresh way. It was during this era that the dramaturge's role was further widened to include translation and adaptation. Leading dramaturges of this period include Gotthold Ephraim Lessing (1729–1781) at the Hamburg National Theatre, and translator of Shakespeare, Ludwig Tieck (1773–1853). The German playwright and critic Johann Wolfgang von Goethe (1749–1832) is also frequently credited with introducing the three essential questions to be used when evaluating a play: what is being attempted? How well is it achieved? Is it worth it? Although the Scottish critic Mark Fisher (1968–2017) more recently attributed these criteria to the lesser-known Italian playwright, Alessandro Manzoni (1785–1873).[3]

In the 20th century, another German, the theatre-maker Berthold Brecht (1898–1956) broadened dramaturgy yet again to include the production, rather than the development of the text alone. The dramaturge now had a remit to research and clarify the political, historical aspects, as well as the form and the aesthetics of a play. In this way, the German dramaturge would participate in rehearsals and in the actualisation of a production.

Figure 4.2 The National Theatre, South Bank, London.

By the mid-1960s, dramaturges were being employed in the Anglophone theatre world but to some extent they have remained synonymous with the position of literary manager. As this guide has revealed, the literary manager and the dramaturge are not one and the same, but a literary manager will normally have dramaturgical responsibilities.

DRAMATURGY TODAY

The most significant recent development in the world of dramaturgy is the publication of Hans-Thies Lehmann's pivotal book, *Postdramatic Theatre* (1999) which endeavours to describe the theatre that has emerged since World War II. Lehmann posited that theatre and drama are now distanced and mutually estranged. Contemporary theatre is certainly, sometimes, fractured, non-linear, immersive, and similar in ways to the internet which has come to dominate the world. Still, by and large, the modern dramaturge remains focused on the play, the emotional experience of the audience, the dramatic structure of the work, and the big idea underpinning a play. There remains some overlap between the role of the literary manager and that of the dramaturge and the dramaturge will sometimes be involved in activities beyond the text such as pre-show talks, blogging, and participating in playwright development schemes – activities which are normally more associated with a literary manager. To confuse matters further, some theatres will refer to the person who runs their literary department as the theatre's dramaturge. More pertinently, in other theatres, the literary manager will be occupied solely with dramaturgy. It's not possible to entirely demarcate these roles when this blurring of responsibilities remains, but it is helpful to look at what dramaturgy always involves.

The role of the dramaturge, or a literary manager whose primary role is to provide dramaturgical advice, will depend greatly on whether the play is newly written, devised, an adaptation, translation, or a revival. Generally speaking, the dramaturge is largely occupied with working with the playwright in honing the various elements of a new text, or researching and advising on aspects of an established text. With an existing text, for example, a dramaturge will supply the director, the cast, and crew with crucial research, context, and interpretation of a play, so that they are best equipped to perform their jobs.

A dramaturge is usually associated with drama, but can equally be involved in a musical, an opera, dance, and choreography, or even, and increasingly these days, digital performance.

Figure 4.3 The Old Vic Theatre, The Cut, London.

PATHS INTO DRAMATURGY

A BA in English or Theatre Studies, and preferably an MA, would be advantageous but it is not an essential requirement. The postgraduate courses listed on page 18 would certainly be worth considering. Many dramaturges have made their name in working behind the scenes in theatre production or were actors or playwrights before making the leap. Some will have been reviewing plays for some years, either for the traditional press, or more recently as a theatre blogger.

Whatever the background, a broad knowledge of arts and humanities helps, and a dramaturge would be expected to have a deep and wide understanding of the dramatic canon. Anyone at the very early stages of contemplating dramaturgy as a career would be well advised to approach their nearest new-writing theatres and offer their services as a reader of unsolicited scripts, or similarly reading for a playwriting competition. In this way, the future dramaturge can work their way up through the ranks of the literary department.

Experience as a writer can help. Dramaturges are sometimes also playwrights themselves or are engaged in other forms of creative, or academic writing. They ought to have an understanding of the process of textual analysis, a proven ability to research and a thorough grasp of craft issues. As with the literary manager, good written and verbal communication skills are also characteristic of the skilled dramaturge. Additionally, it would be necessary that they are team players and are comfortable in collaborative environments. A dramaturge should have the confidence to voice opinions and ask questions that are provoking, but they are always on the playwright/production's side.

Just as a literary manager's responsibilities can vary from theatre to theatre, a dramaturge's job description will change from production to production. On a revival of an established play or a classic text, for example, they will collaborate most closely with the director, researching and understanding the play's context, period and themes, and supplying a sounding board for the director as they work together to solidify a vision and then assist in communicating this interpretation of the work to the cast and crew. If working on a new play, they will be most closely involved with the playwright, giving feedback during the revision process and helping to steer them towards the realisation of their dramaturgical goals. They may also be active in penning programme notes and could be consulted on related marketing material.

Analytical skills are a must. The best dramaturges enjoy dissecting a script and scrutinising and weighing the various elements: plot, structure, language, character, language and dialogue, subtext, genre-specificity, symbolism, imagery, and theme. The dramaturge will consider, pin down and impart the play's subtext and will help identify the characters' intentions. The dramaturge will research and discover as much as they can about the text, the period, language, and previous productions – and share this knowledge.

Figure 4.4 Criterion Theatre and statue of Eros, Piccadilly.

A desirable trait in a dramaturge is diplomacy. A dramaturge will take note of the pecking order within a production, and will know and when and how to proffer advice and share information with the director, and when to hold back and not step on toes. They will impart crucial information or critical notes discretely. The dramaturge should never come between the director and the cast and crew, or cause any disharmony.

If it is necessary that you incisively understand the particular responsibilities of the dramaturge, or literary manager, or literary associate, within a specific institution – it is simply best that you ask the theatre to expressly outline the scope and limits of that distinct role within that institution. As long as there remains debate regarding titles and responsibilities, then asking for such a definition is perfectly acceptable.

Figure 4.5 The Late Dramaturge, Literary Manager, Playwright and Director Donald Howarth (Left), in Conversation with a Writer on the Balcony of His Home, Lower Mall, Hammersmith, London.

THE SPECIFIC RESPONSIBILITIES OF A DRAMATURGE

Much will depend on whether the play is an older text, written by a dead playwright, or a new play by a living writer. In the first instance, the dramaturge will become deeply familiar with the text, reading and re-reading it until they are sure they have grappled with every aspect of the text and have thoroughly analysed it, identifying aspects such as its parentage, and categorising it in terms of genre or genre-crosses. They will then consider the history of the piece, taking into account details about the playwright's life story, experiences, and worldview. Experts on our dramatic past, dramaturges will provide notes on the politics and social commentary under-riding the work. They will research previous productions and access and note criticism of previous productions, and any information surrounding translations of the work. They will then feedback all of this to the director/playwright, this will likely take the form of an exhaustive written statement or report, or even a central production 'bible,' and there will be at least one meeting before rehearsals are launched.

If working with a playwright, it's the dramaturge's job to prompt the writer to think, to consider aspects afresh. The playwright Simon Stephens reflects on his experiences of dramaturgy, detailing the process of the literary manager reading the draft and getting a handle on what he wants to say, what he wants this play to do, maybe even before he is aware of it himself, and helps him achieve it:

> When I'm writing a play, the literary manager or the dramaturge will respond to its early drafts. It's often about pointing out what works, and where you are being self-indulgent. They will advise along those lines and will help define the core, the message of the play, hone the structure, the architecture of the work. That's the scaffolding I need. By providing feedback, they can also help counter a writer's self-doubt. Responding to work in progress is fundamental to the role. Clarity and honesty is crucial.[4]

Literary manager Gavin Kostick agrees and cautions against too much intervention:

> Meet playwrights and discuss their plays. Ask questions but don't dictate to them. Essentially, you are the first audience member. Share your experience of the play with the playwright. Establish what they are trying to do. Consider if this is being well communicated by the work. Discuss what is working in terms of character, structure etc… and highlight areas for improvement. Also, you need to learn how to say 'no'.[5]

Fleur Hebditch views her expertise in dramaturgy as:

> The ability to be able to read a play and visualise it on a stage, imaging how it might work. And knowing what your particular audience wants. And ensuring that this play can take the audience on a journey, and being able to feel that journey – connecting to that. You must be able to spot continuity errors – it's easy for writers to make such mistakes when the creativity is flowing. You should understand how a mood might be created and be able to laugh or cry at a play.[6]

Rebecca Mairs will take time to steer the playwright towards a more succinct understanding of their own play:

> You need to be able to read a play critically, to become an expert on it. You must also engage with and have conversations with writers and learn to ask the right questions so that they are very clear themselves on what the central message of the play is, what the talking point will be in the pub afterwards. I like to lead them to defining it in some way, is it historical, biographical – and if it is, I'll encourage them to do research regarding the era or the setting etc…[7]

Dramaturges are likely to be invited to attend and actively take part in production meetings and rehearsals also, providing guidance on semiotics, costume, accents, period music, period-appropriate art movements, pronunciations, related lighting, and all manner of notes related to the world of the play – especially if this an old play. Guidance on the production will ultimately come from the director, but the dramaturge should have the director's ear.

The dramaturge is the production's first audience and critic. They will dispense notes on these early run-throughs and rehearsals, identifying potential banana skins and moments where an aspect of the play is not reading as it ought, or perhaps not conveying what it might. In addition, the dramaturge may be tasked with keeping a record of the production process and the various production decisions made at various points throughout the rehearsal period – and keeping these notes on file.

When working with a contemporary playwright on a new play, the dramaturge works as a facilitator – or as some say, a midwife. A writer might need help in reigning in and arranging their ideas, distilling them, and focusing them into a script. The dramaturge helps to clarify what the writer wants to say and helps them to say it in a clearer and in a more structured, effective way. A dramaturge is the writer's friend, but one who is not afraid to tell them the truth. Their questioning will elicit the courage of the writer's convictions and ensure they know what it is specifically, they are addressing in their work. For the playwright, the dramaturge is a sounding board and a debating partner, but they ultimately will respect the writer's authorship.

Figure 4.6 Dramaturge Tommo Fowler, at Work.

Tommo Fowler is a freelance dramaturge for text and production, a Supported Artist at Sheffield Theatres, and a Board Member of the Dramaturges' Network. Fowler views the blurring of literary management and dramaturgy from the dramaturge's perspective and reflects on what activities a dramaturge might carry out that a literary manager perhaps would not, and vice versa. He also laments the lack of official or organised support for dramaturges. His frank and detailed insights are highly informative and helpful:

> When we talk about the difference between dramaturges and literary managers, I think uncertainty creeps in because they're both creative roles concerned with the doing of dramaturgy. And in the UK – where the school system frames drama as literature, and text-based theatre reigns supreme – dramaturgical work is also primarily literary work.
>
> It's the management part of the title where the real difference comes in, I think, because it speaks to corporate structures and departments – basically, the internal processes of institutions. It's only building- or company-based dramaturges who are given the title of 'literary manager,' and that institutional position brings with it a whole range of tasks which sit alongside the work of 'doing dramaturgy': these relate to the employing institution's practices for nurturing writers and developing/programming plays for performance.
>
> So, from the perspective of a freelance dramaturge, it seems to me that – on an extremely basic level – to be a literary manager is to be a dramaturge ***and*** an administrator. There are script submission windows to budget for and administrate, reading panels to manage, received scripts to log and disseminate amongst readers, script reports to read and assess, then further steps to plan and action… All of which I simply don't need to worry about as a freelance dramaturge.
>
> Individual theatres may manage this workload slightly differently – many have literary assistants or associates to take on the majority of admin and leave more space for literary managers to do dramaturgy. In these cases, the 'manager' part of the title is also intensely bureaucratic: you're a member of the senior leadership team, with the higher pay-grade and the responsibility for managing other workers that goes with it.
>
> Perhaps this is more informed by my understanding of the role of the dramaturge in continental theatres than it is by actual UK practice, but – when I see a building list a dramaturge on their team rather than a literary manager – I imagine them to be working in a way that extends beyond pure text and into making, to be concerned with the entire visual/aural experience of theatre.

To me, the title of 'dramaturge' suggests a role that's more dynamic, visual, and rooted in the rehearsal room. I'd also expect them to be thinking more about the theatre's place in its geographic and cultural context, and its aesthetic/political/civic aims, and how it fulfils them as an institution in every area of its work – a role that is perhaps more holistic, rather than siloed away with the scripts.

(Of course, there are my own biases and values in my self-identification as a dramaturge! And the literary manager might well occupy any or all of these spaces as well – but perhaps not as a primary duty).

I'm interested that several theatres/companies which have a more 'continental' dramaturgical role (or at least currently employ European artists within it) are those which don't have a literary manager – like the Young Vic or English Touring Theatre, who both employ a 'Creative Associate' to do their dramaturgy, without the sifting of unsolicited scripts and running of reading panels.

Ruth Little is a really interesting outlier in the dramaturge/literary manager binary: she's a former Literary Manager at the National Theatre and Royal Court Theatre, now a dance dramaturge. I don't know many literary managers here who have that fluidity to their work. Literary managers tend to stick with text-based, writer-led theatre, whereas many dramaturgs work consistently across multiple art-forms.

Another other big difference is: most people I know who call themselves dramaturges (as a distinct job, not part of another practice like directing), and who are not literary managers, are precariously employed rather than salaried. Many of them earn a living by teaching in universities, for example, and there's a real shortage of jobs – or opportunities to gain/develop new skills or 'work your way up.'

The career pathways to literary management have tended to be via other creative routes (or via admin roles). Courses with industry experience such as the Leeds Conservatoire MA Dramaturgy might change that in years to come, but it's interesting to note that, although there are (a few) courses for dramaturgy, there are none for literary management – and I don't know many literary managers who are formally trained dramaturges.

As far as official support for dramaturges goes, there's no union for dramaturges – whether in-house or building based. The Writers Guild of Great Britain (WGGB) don't represent dramaturges as distinct creatives – only as writers – and my sense is that there are fears around dramaturges blurring the boundaries of writing credits, with all the questions around IP/royalties that might bring (there was a famous case about this for the musical *Rent*). Understandably, they're protecting their dedicated writers, and I expect would rather that dramaturges who write join their union rather than having their own.

> I'm certainly not with a union as a dramaturg, and I don't know anyone who is. And for what it's worth, I don't know anyone who has an agent specifically for their work as a dramaturge either! So, without the support of a union or HR department, this is another space in which a dramaturge is arguably more precariously employed than a literary manager.[8]

NOTES

1. Magda Romanska, *Routledge Companion to Dramaturgy* (Routledge, London) pp. 1–5.
2. Aristotle, *Poetics,* Part 6(a): The 6 Parts of Tragedy.
3. Mark Fisher, *How to Write About Theatre: A Manual for Critics, Student and Bloggers* (Bloomsbury, Methuen).
4. Sue Healy's Interview with Simon Stephens, London, August 13, 2021.
5. Sue Healy's interview with Gavin Kostick, via Zoom, July 22, 2021.
6. Sue Healy's interview with Fleur Hebditch, via Zoom, July 22, 2021
7. Sue Healy's interview with Rebecca Mairs, via Zoom, August 10, 2021.
8. Sue Healy's interview with Tommo Fowler, via email, April 5, 2022.

CHAPTER 5

Supporting and nurturing new writers

A PASTORAL ROLE

Probably the most significant difference between a literary manager and a dramaturge is the degree to which a literary manager will be involved in mentoring playwrights in terms of their long-term career and growth as a writer, and even their education and development as a person. In addition to the dramaturgical and editorial help they provide for the writer, the literary manager will often act as a blend of therapist, teacher, relationship counsellor, and pastor, and even give direction on practical matters including career and financial advice. The playwright Simon Stephens recalls the life advice he received from Graham Whybrow, then the literary manager at the Royal Court (1994–2007):

> A good [literary manager] will give you broad career advice. Graham encouraged me to travel more to get a different perspective on things. He even suggested that I get a job as a court clerk as I'd get to write down interesting events and meet people I wouldn't normally meet such as lawyers and criminals. I didn't follow up on this, but it was very good advice.[1]

Stephens further outlines what he sees as good practice by a literary manager.

> They should check in on you, but not be too intrusive. I think there needs to be a balance with the literary manager making sure that the playwright doesn't feel forgotten or neglected but at the same time you don't want to feel harassed. Some of it comes down to people skills. Writers should feel valued. The Royal Court does this well in giving tickets to writers and organizing writers' evenings where all writers under commission will go to see the work that the theater is producing. This is good and social and not stressful. It allows people to see the literary manager, but not to feel they're being chased or that anyone is checking up on them.[2]

As Stephens points out, no writer will want to feel hounded. The degree to which you are needed for advice will be up to the playwright themselves, and how appropriate you consider your assistance and direction to be in the matter at hand. Some playwrights will actually want to be left alone and will resent any intrusion into their lives – and this stance must be respected. Others will need pretty consistent attention and reassurance and will come to you with all manner of problems for you to solve. Most playwrights will fall between those two descriptions. It will greatly depend on the character of the playwright and how much help you feel comfortable providing. What is important in the first instance is that you as literary manager and the playwright have an initial conversation about how you plan to work together and agree on some pathway forwards, and you make it clear what you will not be providing.

Some of these playwrights will be young, in their late teens or early twenties and you'll be viewed in *loco parentis*, as they might see a teacher or university lecturer. It is important to have clear boundaries in place and ensure that you act appropriately and responsibly and don't abuse your power.

From what I have observed, literary managers tend to be very empathetic people and if any have ever caused offence by not replying to a query or request, it is likely due to an entirely unintended oversight caused by significant demands on their time. However, theatres are perhaps guilty of forever chasing the next big thing, and in its pursuit, writers that they have encouraged and fostered previously can be overlooked. Thought should be given to how this attitude might impact these writers. This neglect is never meant as a personal slight, nonetheless, the literary manager should be aware that it can be perceived as such, and efforts should be made to keep in touch with their writers, old and new.

Simon Farquhar, a playwright, screenwriter, crime writer, and novelist, generously provides a thorough, honest, and very instructive account of his experiences with literary managers from the beginning of his career through a remarkable success, and then the aftermath of that success. His encounters with the profession run the gamut from good, through to what he perceives as the bad or indifferent literary manager.

I appreciate Farquhar's frankness and willingness to talk about the negative impact of what he perceived as radio silence from a literary department to which he was attached. I include his viewpoint not to criticise a colleague or a theatre, after all every literary manager, myself included, will have upset a playwright at some point,

Figure 5.1 Simon Farquhar, Playwright.

usually completely unwittingly. I cite Farquhar's perception of his experience because it presents how a lack of engagement might be interpreted even if this is not the intent, and he reveals the impact that impression can subsequently have on the writer and their career. Playwrights are sometimes reluctant to grouse publically about what they feel was shoddy treatment, for fear of not getting future work on, or that they'll be viewed as merely disgruntled over a rejection. So, accounts like Farquhar's are rare in print, and as such they're valuable and educational for the literary manager. I am grateful to Farquhar for having the courage to be so honest and candid. His reflections might perhaps help literary managers appreciate the power that is in their hands, and to consider the means it is deployed, and how to apply strategies to ensure all writers connected with their theatre feel valued.

A VIEW FROM A PLAYWRIGHT

> When I started out, I didn't really know exactly really what a literary manager was. It was a title I saw on old arts documentaries and particularly from watching programmes on the Royal Court and that sort of thing. So, I got a sense that it was a sort of midwife between the playwright and the eventual production. They became, in my head, people that you desperately wanted to corner and sweet talk. In my experience, it was always very much that the onus was on you to seek out those people, no one ever seemed to be touting for business and saying we're

looking for writers for X, Y, and Z. And at that time, when I was starting out, the theatres I went to the most were the Bush and the Court. I saw everything that they did, absolutely everything, over a five-year period. This would have been in the early 2000s. There was never any sense that "we're looking for playwrights," there always seemed to be more than was needed, so you had to find your own way.

I remember the early days of sending stuff off, before I had an agent, you'd very occasionally get something back from a literary department. It was very rarely the literary manager of a place, usually the assistant. You used to get a standard letter. I was always quite depressed by the feedback because I never found it was constructive, it always felt quite tokenistic. They would always begin with a compliment, "This was a good read, bla bla bla." You'd get the sense that they're just thinking, "well, I need to say something to this person." Quite often the feedback they offered was just that "you could have done it this way instead." There was never any suggestion that "this will make it better." It used to infuriate me, telling me I could have done it another way instead. Yeah, I know, but I did it this way, so tell me what is wrong with that? I always thought that that paragraph giving you guidance was never used in its proper way. It antagonises you and it's quite disheartening.

The truth is that every play can have a suggestion thrown at it, and if a theatre wants to do it, they'll take it on however much work it might need. I remember the first time actually meeting a literary manager properly when they became interested in me. The first literary manager I dealt with was at the Soho Theatre and that was Nina Steiger. I'd written my first full length stage play. I'd had a few things on and one thing published, but they were short things, in Scotland. Then I wrote this play called *Spin The Bottle* and my agent hawked it around and suddenly, he called me and he said, "I've got you this meeting, at Soho theatre." It was an incredible feeling. It's like you're trying to get into a castle and suddenly you're at the battlements. I met Nina Steiger. You're slightly in awe of the fact that this person holds so many people's destinies in their hands, it's extraordinary. She was the person that I dealt with. We sat and had a coffee and she talked about the play. She was very good, very enthusiastic and she seemed to take me seriously. I felt like I was being interviewed as a writer rather than someone who wanted to be a writer. What was interesting was that she didn't want to do the play, but she was interested in me.

Nina said that the Verity Bargate Award was coming up soon and it would be really good if I could enter something in that. It turned out that it was closing in nine days. I thought I couldn't say no. It so happened at the time that I did have an idea about a one-night stand that leads to an obsession. It was all tied up with experiences that I'd had observing life around me when I lived in Scotland. I ran the opening scene by her – a one-night stand, shown in real time. She got really into this idea and said that I should definitely go off and do this. So, I did. I wrote the play in eight days. It was already beginning to take shape in some ways. It wasn't difficult, it was really ten years of my life recalled and squeezed into it. Everyone wondered if it was autobiographical, it wasn't. Most of it was true, but it hadn't happened to me, it had happened in the world around me. I sent that off to the Verity Bargate. It didn't win and we never heard any more from Nina Steiger. I think she did come back and say she really liked it, but we never heard any more after that. I learned then the first lesson of nothing is set in stone. Suddenly you just stop getting replies to things, and that is really a hard knock. You leave with your head full of dreams and then nothing happens, and it's not like you even get a letter saying that they're not interested anymore, they just forget about you.

My agent was really keen on *Rainbow Kiss*, and he hawked it around and entered it into the George Devine Award for promising playwrights. It ended up nearly winning, they created a 'runner up' placing for it. I was then asked to go to the award presentation of the George Devine Award at the Royal Court in Sloane Square. I didn't have a clue what it was all about. When I turned up to this thing, which was at a daft time like noon. I thought no one would be there. I turned up and everybody and their dog was there, all these people whose names I knew from theatre programmes and stuff. Everyone there had all read my play and they were all talking to me about it and saying, "obviously they're going to do it, aren't they, the Court?" I didn't have any forewarning of this at all. I hadn't met anyone from the Court or anything. So, I came in through a backdoor.

Shortly after that, I was called in to see Graham [Whybrow] the literary manager at the time. I sat in this room surrounded by all these files with all these names of famous playwrights on them. It was a surreal feeling. What was different about my meeting was that, as compared to other people's experiences, the play itself wasn't really talked about that much. I suppose it was considered to be a complete entity. It had already achieved something by being this runner-up in the George Devine Award. They never really suggested any changes. They were just interested in me. But because I was not as young as most of the new playwrights they find, I think they were all just a bit baffled as to who I was, what my story was and where I'd come from, and what they ought to with me.

To be honest, when I met them first, I was probably very wary of giving them honest answers because I didn't want to blow it. I felt I needed to make myself sound a bit more interesting and more Royal Court-y than I was. I'm sure all the other writers do the same though. Perhaps that's why Royal Court writers used to seem so edgy until you actually met them.

I used to go and see Graham quite a lot because I liked him and I found him fascinating, full of insight, dispensing pearls of wisdom and that sort of stuff. It was only the second time I went in when they commissioned it. It was Graham and Ian Rickson in the office. Ian was the artistic director at that time. They went round the houses a bit, which is a Royal Court technique, and then said "well, we'd like to do it." I just gasped, I was overwhelmed. And there it was, on the programme for the Royal Court's 50th anniversary, in the anniversary slot.

There was barely any literary discussion. That mostly came afterwards, during rehearsals, from the director and cast. Ian Rickson said something about being careful with protagonists who are emoting a lot, that they can lose the audience's sympathy and he noted some good examples of getting around it, with *Lear, Hamlet,* and *Uncle Vanya*. But all that happened at the end was that it was cut down a little bit. My proper dealings with the Court, in particularly dealing with the literary manager, came with the second commission. And by then there was a new literary manager.

The thing was that although when you are new to a world, you don't know what should and shouldn't be the case. I did feel by then that I'd been very much left to it, and I was a bit stranded. There was very much a pool of people at the Court who were the 'in' writers under Ian Rickson's tenure: Leo Butler, Simon Stephens, and Lucy Prebble. They were younger than me, most of them were anyway. I came in at the tail end of Ian's time as artistic director and sometimes felt a bit like I'd been rescued off the streets, whereas the others had been nurtured over several years. I remember as a company with *Rainbow Kiss*, we felt very much the outsiders. I never really felt that the Court were particularly into it. Ian only came to the first preview. They never updated the ticket booking line from what had been on before us. I felt that they had to do because it was a new play that had been bigged up, and it was the 50th anniversary and they saw it as a bit *Look Back in Anger*-y, but there wasn't really a great deal of support, not really. Looking back now, I should have been fostered and nurtured a bit more. They did commission a second one, for downstairs, which was quite scary. I completely screwed up because I got second album syndrome. I worried about it far too much. I remember also, and this is important, that after the final performance, my girlfriend and I stood and watched the set being axed down, and I remember thinking that no one was there to give you any kind of well-wish or remind you that you are still under the Court's wing. Also, the set had featured a lot of records and books, which I'd been asked to supply, and I was then told to come and collect them on Monday morning, and there they were, just dumped in a corridor and no arrangements for how I was meant to get them home. You felt a bit like your suitcases were on the pavement.

I remember going to see [the literary manager] Graham [Whybrow] in the early stages of writing the second play and talking to him about it. He was really good. I said I've got this idea. I know the world I want to write about and stuff, but I'm having this problem because I can't work out how to physically do it. There is too much going on, there are too many realms. It was really a leap from a very intimate chamber piece into something that is huge, and I don't really like big plays. I like intimate pieces. I much prefer a smaller, more concentrated thing. I remember that Graham got some paper and did a little diagram, a little sketch of an example of how you can do a certain thing on stage, intimately, but incorporating a lot. It wasn't "this is how you should do it," it was "this is an example of the fact that anything can be done." Graham always used to come out with these little aphorisms, like: "art is a revenge for life" or "you can't use art to settle old scores" and all that (I always thought they rather contradicted each other, but there you go). I always found Graham very inspiring. He had a huge knowledge of what he was doing and always appeared very interested in you in a non-judgmental way. It was as if he treated people a little like plays, in the sense that he studies them and draws from them a little bit. I found that endearing – though it wouldn't suit everyone. All that I used to find very valuable and very useful, but I never felt that there was a particularly engaged conversation about my play. And then Graham left the literary manager position, after 14 years there.

A new literary manager arrived and made no effort to contact me, never asked me how it was going or anything like that. So of course, I ended up spending ridiculous amounts of time over-writing and over-thinking the piece. I didn't actually meet the new literary manager until I delivered the play. They absolutely hated it. We had a very frosty meeting. When I look back on it now, I see that the play was a complete mess, but within it, there's still something I'm very proud of. Really what they should have done, was to have said to me, "you need to lift the heart of this out and put it into a different format, because it's not a stage play in its current form." But they never said that, they just rejected it outright, which I felt was a bit of a waste considering they'd paid me for it. It left me rather disheartened with the whole thing. After that, I just retreated away. I felt very much like I had a great future behind me, because when you have a little success like that, and everybody likes it and everybody is saying nice things to you, and suddenly there you are and you think "that was my moment and it's gone." I didn't go into the Court for over a year after that. I got extremely upset by it all. I remember going then to see something much later and seeing the literary manager at the bar but I didn't have the confidence to say: "Can you help me, please? This theatre put me on a path, and I'm really lost now, can you help?" I didn't,

I just skulked away. It became this ludicrous process whereby, because I was still on the sort of Court's writers' list, I'd get invites for everything and go, and I'd always get "What are you up to now?" from the literary people. I'd go, "Well, I sent you a play and you've not read it." One of them used to actually laugh at it as if it was some sort of running joke.

What is interesting is that during that wilderness period, when the Court had a new literary manager and I was abandoned to write the play and was having a very tough time, I actually bumped into the Court's old literary manager, Graham Whybrow, in a pub. I was really at a low ebb and I did sort of pour my heart out to Graham. He asked me what the problem was with the play and gave me some advice. He also gave me a list of places I could approach to solicit some financial support, to see me through. Remember, I'd given up my job and everything to write for the Court, and by now, I was struggling. I walked out of that pub feeling very positive. I remember going straight home and finishing the play, in fact. And also on Graham's suggestion, I wrote to and obtained some money from the Peggy Ramsay Foundation. I remember feeling that I wished that I'd had a chance to work with Graham from beginning to end on a project and that this was the sort of support I should have been getting from the Court, and from the literary manager who was *in situ* at the time, not their former literary manager I'd just randomly met in a pub. So, I finished that play, sent it off, and they never read it.

I could say that I've met three distinct types of literary managers in my career, an inspiring and helpful one, one I found unsupportive and not available, and others I've felt were disinterested. The latter is the kind of literary manager who basically finds it amusing that you're always asking them to read your play, which is just terrible. So, I mean, I remember just having a very a glimpse of a great literary manager in Graham, and then the rough end of another immediately afterwards. The great one is the one that says, "if you think about it this way, it can be done," compared to the one who says simply "No, game over." And the disinterested one who more or less says "who are you? I'm far too busy to read plays like yours."

Having seen what literary managers are capable of, and what you as a writer want when you're working, one of the things that I think is good for a literary manager to organise is a sort of social dimension to the theatre, a monthly talk or the like. I think when you're a writer and you go to the theatre, and it's not your play, you feel a strange sense of exclusion. Whereas if you go to the theatre with a group of other writers, a meeting that the theatre has put together for you, you feel under that wing and valued, and that is really good.

Another issue is that theatres can be very ageist. I remember the Court saying to me, "Oh, you're too old for the young writers' programme," and me thinking, "well, then, why have a *young* writers' programme, why not just a writers' programme?" It's ridiculous. Theatres are prejudiced in other ways too. As an example, I can remember sitting in a literary manager's office once, who was complaining how arduous it was to have to go through all the unsolicited scripts. This literary manager then picked up a script with a cover letter and said, "look at this," and read out the address despairingly, as if where it had come from was the ultimate paralyzing suburban place and no good writing could ever come from there. I said, quite truthfully, "that's actually the road I grew up on."

I'm bewildered and in awe of 19-year-olds who can write incredible plays. I didn't have anything interesting to say at 19. I thought I did, but I definitely didn't. But I would quite like to know what a 65-year-old woman has got to say, no matter what her background. And those people, they're not getting plays put on, whether they're submitting them or not, I don't know but they're certainly not being reached out to. I do find this a little bit depressing. If new writing in theatres is something which is specifically for the young, then where does everybody go afterwards? If they've had any success, they'll go to television. The theatres then say, "Oh they've gone off to television, isn't that terrible," but they do little to keep them in theatre.

Literary managers I've noticed, at least all the ones I've met and spoke to socially, like to be able to say afterwards that they were the literary manager at the time when so-and-so came through. Obviously, that's irresistible to be able to say that you were there and you were presiding over that sort of thing. At the same time, they might say, "you don't fit in with the movement that we're championing at the moment." I think that's a shame. I used to find, quite often, in particular back in the early 00s, that the plays were quite interchangeable. Not just because of that style at the time, but, you know, because of the literary manager was leaning towards the same thing all the time and it gets a bit same-y.

And I am always fascinated to hear literary managers talk to you about plays that they've put on that they actually thought were rubbish. So, if you pluck up the courage say, "I really didn't think that that was very good," and they say, "oh, it was awful, wasn't it?" I'm always left wondering, why on earth did you programme it? If you ask, they'll say of course, "well, it was because we've done everything else by him, or because so-and-so wanted to do it." Try telling that to some poor bloke who has had ten rejections from that theatre. It's grim.

It would be nice to know that there is somewhere you can pick the phone up and have a chat and say "I'm a writer, you're a literary manager, can we meet for coffee?" Writing is a lonely and solitary thing to do and to be able to talk to someone about it is always good. I don't know what it's like for other people, but when I hand something over, I will be confident that I've done my best with it but I will have no idea of how it will read to someone else. As soon as that person has read it, the literary manager or whoever, and they start referring to the events or the characters of it, it becomes exciting, real. That's a precious process. I don't think enough is made of that moment. If a play is being read, and there is any sort of future to it, the literary manager should look for the writer to come in and talk to them. Writers need loving and they need looking after, I don't think it goes on nearly enough.

Also, the rejection thing, I loathe that tokenistic "it could have been more this." It's better to ask a question in a rejection letter than to make a statement. That's what a literary manager surely should always be doing, is questioning. You would never go in with your writer and tell them what to think and what to do.

I entirely appreciate that literary manager is in a job which is underfunded and over stretched, but I feel the commissioned writer should have regular meetings with a literary manager, like you might regularly meet your manager in the workplace. My experience, the idea of being abandoned for two years to write a play, and then just getting a flat rejection, well, that wasn't a good experience. It shouldn't have happened. I appreciate that the ethos of the job is to find stories and to find people with urgent and exciting things to say and all that, but you do need to also nurture the writers you have.

It's a bit of a wilderness to make your way around and if you're a writer you are insecure because you are hesitant about the world, I suppose. So, I always felt I wish I'd known a little bit more than about the rights and wrongs because now I see that there were things that should have been done, but weren't. In a sense, I am an example of what not to do and also what a literary manager shouldn't do. I've always suspected that because the Court didn't specifically discover me, that my play came into view via the George Devine Award and not through a submission process at the Royal Court, I suffered because of that. There was a sense I was foisted on them, I think, and that I was accepted begrudgingly only because some people, important but peripheral people, thought the Court *should* do the play. I think this was part of the reason I didn't get an enormous amount of support there.

Everybody in the arts says that they are excited to work with you, and then don't answer your calls of letters. And it should not happen. It's rude. You end up feeling completely rejected. It's horrible. It's a working environment but this wouldn't happen in other workplaces.

I was always very drawn to the older generation. They probably felt that I was more their kind of writer, people like Anthony Page, Ted Whitehead, and Donald Howarth. I always used to find them inspirational and I learned a lot from them. I used to seek them out. I loved listening to their war stories and hearing about their battle scars. I remember Ted Whitehead saying that he'd been warned that the Court was like the mafia, but he found it was nothing like that, that it didn't have that clan loyalty, "it was actually more like working with the Borgias," he said.

I had a very good friend, the late great TV director Claude Watham. Claude had had a lifetime's experience of working with and dealing with writers and he knew how writers functioned. He said once said to me when I'd had something rejected and was a bit glum, he said: "you must understand, Simon, that everyone in the arts and in the media, they only work for themselves. Every decision that they make is based on how it will benefit them." He didn't mean this in a castigating way. What he meant was if a TV producer or a theatre's literary manager reads a script and decides not to progress it, it doesn't necessarily mean that it's a terrible script, it means that it's not the next stepping stone that they see on their career. You should never be disheartened by rejection. If a literary manager turns down a writers' work, it isn't necessarily because it's lacking in value, it's because they don't think they can or want to take the theatre in that direction. I've always remembered that.[3]

Figure 5.2 Simon Farquhar, Playwright.

WAYS TO MENTOR WRITERS

It's crucial to continue to be plain, direct, and unambiguous with writers and to manage their expectations. Especially if the writer is new to the profession, a simple coffee and chat with the literary manager may quickly encourage dreams of having their work on the main stage within months. Whereas the reality is that the literary manager sees promise in their voice and would like to steer them onto a suitable path, give them the tools to feed their talent to reach its potential but it's unlikely they're planning to programme work any time soon. It's key that the writer is not spurred into indulging any unrealistic expectations – as this will lead to disappointment and ill-feeling down the line. If you are not planning on producing the submitted play, state this very clearly from the outset. Stephens makes this clear:

> Clarity and honesty is crucial. I think it's Mark Ravenhill who says that 'no' is the second best answer, after yes. It's clear and you know where you stand and. You don't waste time. Rejection is hard but it can make you a better writer. My first commission by the Royal Court was rejected, but it made me strive to do better.[4]

Be distinct when outlining what they might expect to gain from the experience and unequivocal in explaining you'd like to be part of that nurturing process and that this is why you are inviting the writer in to talk about the possibilities. Don't promise anything that cannot be delivered.

You might start by offering some dramaturgical support and mentorship, and even perhaps explaining what this might entail (don't assume any knowledge of the process from the new writer). If you decide to offer the writer a development opportunity, ensure that the brief is clearly defined. They should know exactly what they can expect to have achieved at the end of the period. You may well consider giving the writer the time, space, and opportunity to "write the play they've always wanted to write." However, there are always aspects and sensible limitations worth pointing out, even if you think they may be obvious. Let the writer know that, for your theatre, certain approaches and genres won't be realistic (i.e. if yours is a tiny venue, a cast of 50 won't work. If your theatre has a reputation for leaning into urban grit and provocative subject matter, a cosy conservative play set in a rural vicarage is not going to appeal). It is at this early point that the writer should be informed of these parameters, and not when they've travelled to the destination already.

Sit down with the writer and discuss details such as target audience, cast, and length. It is a good idea to draw up some form of the written agreement, even if the playwright is un-agented as yet. Putting down in writing what you both want from the process will ensure that there is no misunderstanding regarding your expectations, deadlines, the extent, and limit of support they might receive from you and the theatre, and how feedback will be provided. At this point, discuss the fee involved

Figure 5.3 Criterion New Writing Program, Financed by the Criterion Theatre Trust.

and how this might be paid. Make sure that the writer understands all in full, any grey areas are potential future headaches. Explain that the writer might later wish to deviate from their original idea, but should this occur, it must be discussed with the literary manager at the earliest possible point. Opportunities will depend on the size of your literary department and what funding you might have at hand. Still, even the smallest, unfunded theatres can foster a culture of development. Here are some suggestions:

ORGANISING WORKSHOPS

If you are mentoring more than one playwright, it is a good idea to have some group involvement. Here you can introduce writers to the various approaches to playwriting via activities and read-throughs of scenes. In this way, the writers will get space to consider all the different aspects that go into writing a play: subtext, dialogue, theme, the big idea, story, form and structure, characters – and more.

All literary managers will be involved in delivering workshops at some point. This activity might be connected with some community engagement programme, for example, visits to schools, or youth groups, or prisons. For this reason, part two of this guide focuses solely on suggested activities for these occasions.

RUNNING UP A WRITERS GROUP

Setting up a writers' group is as simple as inviting a group of playwrights to meet regularly at a venue to read, share, support, and feedback on each other's work. As a literary manager, you might want to lead such a group, and perhaps run workshops on different aspects of playwriting.

Next step is finding somewhere to meet. Of course, in this (hopefully) post-pandemic world, we are all so much more open to Zooming and meeting online, so an IRL venue is not as essential to a writers group as it may once have been. Nonetheless, it may be more appealing to meet in person, occasionally at least. You may be able to use the theatre's rehearsal spaces for this purpose or if your theatre is large enough, you'll possibly have rooms allocated for the meeting already. If there isn't a room or space available to you, do consider a local pub. There is often a function room above the bar, which a friendly landlord might make available to you for an hour or so, if you offer to encourage participants to buy a drink at the bar. This arrangement is quite common in the theatre world. There is a London-based writers' meeting founded by some senior Royal Court writers, they call themselves The Antelopes because they meet in an upstairs room at a Belgravian pub of that name. Always be open to going online if meeting physically proves difficult, it is better that some meeting takes place than none at all.

Think about giving the group a name, it aids the sense of belonging. Your monthly gathering might be called after your theatre – but be mindful that this association will also make all members *de facto* ambassadors for your venue, and this status might carry reputational risk. Alternatively, you might name the group after your geographic location, post code, or provide some name that aligns with the ethos or

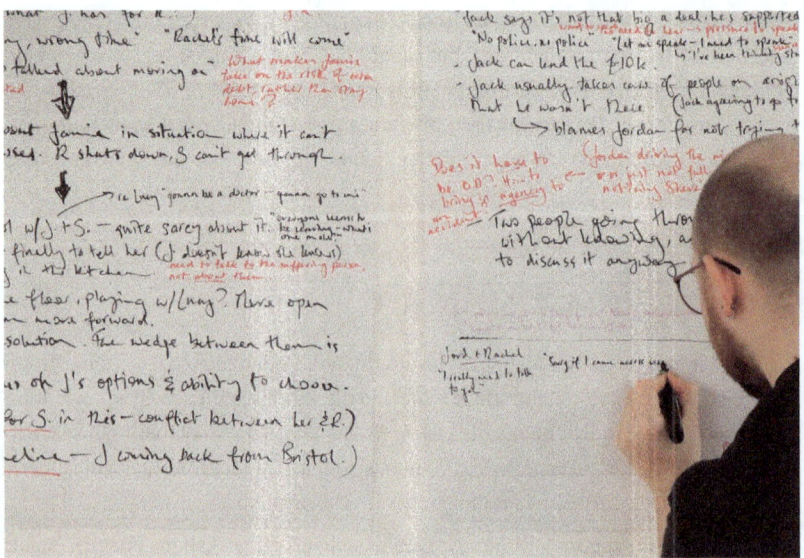

Figure 5.4 Dramaturgy in Action.

goals of the group. How these sessions are run and what shape and mission they have very much depends on your vision, the number of members, and the amount of funding available to you. Here are some suggestions.

START A SOCIAL GROUP LINKED TO YOUR VENUE

You might think about launching an informal social occasion for writers you're nurturing. Writing is, after all, a lonely business and it's good to meet and chat socially with other writers from time to time. It's important for the mental health of your writers, in fact. A social group also allows them to network within their peer group. It fosters confidence and provides a supportive and safe social space, in turn allowing them to move with greater ease within the theatre world later on. As a literary manager, such a group will help you to get to know the young writers socially and it helps you all to bond as a group.

As a literary manager, you will find yourself directing and choreographing the evening. Some writers are naturally gregarious and will socialise and find a company easily. It's the ones that hover on the edges that you'll have to watch and encourage. Keep an eye out for those who aren't joining in the conversation, and see if you can coax them to do so by engaging them in light banter and introducing them all round. Make sure everyone is taking to someone. If participants don't know each other, you could suggest some sort of speed-dating type activities whereby they have a set time to introduce themselves to the others in the group – but do read the room, some writers would loathe this type of ice-breaking activity.

The theatre world can intimidate and draw out insecurity. As a result, some attendees will inflate their importance and achievements, others will withdraw into themselves and down-play their achievements. As a literary manager, try to even it all out and big people up where needed. Where possible, it might be an idea to have a few topics on hand to fuel discussion, and ensure the conversation keeps flowing. Use small talk, it has a very useful purpose in situations like this and will help put all at ease. Resist the temptation to showcase your own knowledge. Perhaps steer clear of any overly divisive topic on first meetings, informally draw out views on a current issue that is having an impact on theatre, or discuss a play that's receiving a bit of traction (or indeed, a TV drama or movie). It's of paramount importance that you put attendees at ease.

It may be a good idea to have these gatherings in the early evening, where people can drop in on their way back from work – and won't be coming along a bit worse for wear from earlier drinks. As always, alcohol will oil the social wheels at these gatherings but if you leave it until later on in the evening, the event could get quite sloppy with that oil.

Set a time for the official meeting, say an hour or 90 minutes, and wrap it at that time. If you and/or other attendees want to keep on partying, that's fine, but don't let it be a feature of your meeting proper. Keep your official gathering tidy, and bring it to an official close at a particular time.

> #Metoo
>
> Since the advent of the #metoo movement, theatres have become more aware of their responsibility in terms of safeguarding staff, and this duty of care extends to writers' gatherings and social events at your theatre. You obviously don't want your writers' meeting to facilitate any harassment or abuse of power. Perhaps include a "code of conduct" in the template of your group correspondence, making it clear that certain behavior will not be tolerated. At the event, keep a casual eye on all corners of the room and if you suspect someone is coming close to bothering or harassing another participant, discretely intervene and check everyone is ok. Remember, as enjoyable as you want these occasions to be, the welfare of the participants and the reputation of you and your theatre will be at risk if you allow lines to be crossed. Have fun, but be watchful and prudent and ensure nothing untoward happens on your watch.

HOLD INDUSTRY TALKS

In 2018, The Finborough Theatre's then playwright on attachment, Carmen Nasr, and I, set up the Finborough Forum. We established this happening as an event where industry figures could be invited to give a talk on a specific aspect of the business to a room full of aspiring and established playwrights from everywhere. The only criterion for attending is that you are a playwright. The evening was initially held in the Finborough Arms pub (a separate entity to the theatre) once a month, and it moved online during the COVID-19 pandemic – where it still takes place. We structured the Forum to include a 30-minute interview and then a further 30 minutes during which guests answer questions from the floor. Initially, after the meeting ended, all attendees were invited to stay on for a further hour to socialise if they so wished – but we lost this element of the evening with the move online. So far, the event has proved very popular. It remains a very good balance of the informative, educational, and the social, and it's fun. We've done our best to ensure we invited industry speakers from across the theatre landscape and guests have included the playwrights Simon Stephens, April de Angelis, James Graham, David Ireland, Anders Lustgarten, and Marina Carr; the agents Mel Kenyon and Alexander Cory, the director Garry Hynes; the screenwriting consultant Philip Shelley; the critics Michael Billington, Aleks Sierz, and Megan Vaughan; the academics Dan Rebellato and Lynette Goddard – to name but a tiny few. It has proven a tremendous success.

Figure 5.5 Neil McPherson, Artistic Director, Finborough Theatre.

Once Carmen and I established the event, the Forum received a small amount of funding from the George Goetchius and Donald Howarth Society of Friends Award, which permitted us to pay a nominal amount to the speakers, enough so that we could at least cover their transport costs and make sure they had enough left over to buy a drink or two on the evening.

If you apply for and secure funding, you'll be able to book guests of a higher industry standing. In your search for funding, do approach charitable trusts who favour the theatre industry, or have an association with your neighbourhood, or figures connected to your theatre. A suggested amount to pay a speaker for such an evening could start at, say, £50 and go up to £500+, depending on how big the event and how celebrated the speaker, where your theatre is and how far a speaker may have to travel, and if they'll need accommodation provided.

Figure 5.6 Fortune Theatre, London.

OBTAINING FUNDING FOR EVENTS

Become acquainted with the charity commission's website:

https://register-of-charities.charitycommission.gov.uk, which lists all active charities in Britain and details their income and area of special interest, trustees, and contact details. Search for charities that sponsor all things theatre and writing related. You might also try for charities that have a particular connection with your area, or arts education, or perhaps a particular demographic with whom you'll be engaging. You will need to know if your own theatre is also a registered charity, as some trusts will only donate to other charities. It might be a good idea to buy a copy of the *Directory of Grant Making Trusts*, which will provide more funding sources. This book is published yearly and the latest copy can be expensive (circa £150.00), so if your budget is tight, opt for a copy a few years out of date. It will probably be just as useful and will cost just a few pounds online. Better still, check your local library, they are bound to have a current edition.

When seeking funding, don't use the entire letter to detail how poor and needy is your theatre with its leaky roof and poor box-office sales. This may be true, but an overdose of negativity doesn't usually appeal and it won't make you an attractive investment. It is fine to say that these are challenging times and funds don't currently stretch to funding renowned guests to appear at your speaker event. However, keep the rest of the letter positive and upbeat and outline what could be done if this money were to be made available. State why this event is foundational to your playwrights' development, and for the theatre community.

If any of your playwrights have had a recent success, be sure to mention, and ditto you or your theatre (think awards, productions, publications, transfers, and rave reviews). Be explicit in how you see any funding producing further positive outcomes. Always, provide a very clear and detailed outline of how the money would be spent, and state on what specifically (a table is useful). Ask for a sum in advance, for example, 12 months. If you are with a larger theatre with an in-house accountant, detailing expenditure is a chore you can easily delegate. For a smaller operation, the following sample outline would probably suffice.

Ensure you communicate clearly why you believe the charity you are approaching might consider supporting your event. Outline what is in it for them (publicity, community good will, an opportunity to promote their work, etc.). Be polite, professional, business-like and brief, and don't waffle or try to fudge any aspect.

If they say no, accept the decision politely and don't argue or complain that they have wasted your time. The charity may have already promised funds elsewhere or may feel that this particular project doesn't align with their objectives at this point. Respect their decision. After you thank them for their time, you could politely ask for feedback and if you could potentially approach them at a future date. Most will be very open to this and might provide some helpful advice on how to get your application over the line in the next round. You need allies not enemies.

If you are lucky enough to be successful in your funding bid, always follow up with a note of gratitude and a short report on how it all went – indeed, this aspect is often a requirement. Remember that those running charities want to find deserving homes for their funds – but they have to justify all donations to the other trustees and

Amount per Month	Purpose	Total Requested for 2023
£100.00	Speakers' fee – includes transport costs	
£20.00	Admin fee for office use	
£50.00	Fee for chairperson	
£10.00	2 promotional T-shirts	
TOTAL *per month*: £180.00		£180 × 12 = £2,160.00 **TOTAL *per annum*: £2,160.00**

the Charity Commission, so help them by supplying clear justification for the grant, and provide nice, succinct detail. Ensure they appreciate you and your theatre, and you'll be more likely to get funding from this source again.

THE IMPORTANCE OF CLARITY AND MANAGING EXPECTATIONS

Mentoring the emerging writer can be offering informal feedback on the finished script, or more structured, regular, and even interventionist. If an emerging writer is offered some form of attachment, residency, or mentoring at your theatre, I recommend setting out clear-eyed expectations from the off.

In the first instance, have a frank discussion with the writer and find out what they want and be equally as candid regarding what you can and can't provide. Be clear and explicit about what you and the theatre would like to gain from this partnership. Don't leave any aspect unspoken, as this will return to haunt. If there is no plan or promise to stage the play, or if this eventuality is a possibility but is in no way guaranteed, make sure the writer fully understands this situation. You may want to keep the writer as excited, enthusiastic, and engaged as could be – but they'll be deeply unhappy and disappointed with you and your theatre if they feel they've been given a false impression from the off. Again, it is advisable to draw up a contract of some description, incorporating how both you and the writer expect to benefit from this mentorship, and this will form the basis and structure of meetings going forward.

Ensure you both agree on how this mentorship will be delivered and in what way, and at what intervals. You can have a template approach, but adapt it to fit the needs and requirements of the individual.

FUNDING MENTORSHIP

Whether or not you can provide a stipend during the mentoring period will depend on the funding available to you/your theatre. It is highly advisable that you explore various means to provide this support. If a writer is going to devote, say, six months to crafting a play – then it is likely they will have to step back from their regular work to do so, to some extent at least. Most writers will have rents to pay, children to feed, and loans to pay off – so they will need to be compensated for the loss of earnings if they are going to devote a significant amount of time to a project linked to your theatre. Thankfully, there are some grants already in existence that may help:

> **The Channel 4 Playwrights Scheme** awards six bursaries of £10,000 each year to playwrights being mentored by a theatre. Previous recipients include major British and Irish talents including: Martin McDonagh, Nancy Harris, Simon Stephens, Joe Penhall, Laura Wade, Winsome

Pinnock, Richard Bean, Tanika Gupta, Hanif Kureishi and Lucy Prebble, to name but a few. Four bursaries are supported by Channel 4, and two by the Peggy Ramsay Foundation. In addition, the Sonia Friedman Productions Award is given to the writer of the best play written by one of the previous year's bursary recipients. Contact details

The Peggy Ramsay Foundation can be approached directly to apply for funding to afford dramatists the time and space to write. Financial assistance will not exceed £5,000, and is normally significantly less, so this award might work best in a small portfolio of grants for your writer. www.peggyramsayfoundation.org

The Arts Council of England /Wales/Northern Ireland and Creative Scotland will provide grants for playwrights working on a specific project. Your theatre can apply, or you can assist the individual playwright in their own application. Applying for grants can be an arduous, complicated and a confusing process – but in my experience it is always worth giving the Council a call. They genuinely want to give money to artists and arts institutions, and despite the impression created by all the off-putting form filling, you'll normally find a warm and helpful voice on the other end of the line. An Arts Council advisor will readily provide application councel and steer you in the right direction. In Ireland, the system differs both in terms of application approach, structure and what type of funding is available, and when, but the core idea is the same and if you seek help and advice on how to apply, you'll receive sterling direction freely.

As always, when writing the proposal don't over egg the pudding in terms of how needy and poor your theatre or the playwright is, rather focus on the positives and potential of investment in this project/artist, and supply a detailed budget and a clear and detailed potential time-table from beginning to end.

Artscouncil.org.uk
Arts.wales
Creativescotland.com
Artscouncil-ni.org
Artscouncil.ie

I'll list below further organisations known for providing support to theatres and/or playwrights. Give time to researching. Explore all the websites to see which might match with your specific funding needs. I'd advise you to also find out about grants available to people in your precise location, your local arts officer might help here. Pay close attention to the individual criteria for each trust and charity and make sure

Figure 5.7 The Globe Theatre, London.

you (or the playwright you're mentoring) ticks every box before applying. Whilst you will likely have a template grant application letter, each application will have to be adapted to suit the requests, requirements, and demands of the specific trust or foundation. Consider what aspect of the project (or the playwright, or your theatre) might specifically appeal to the charity in focus, and give this aspect centre stage in your application. If you send an application on without the appropriate tweaking, it will be obvious that you didn't provide the research, time, and focus you ought to have given the application process. Although such a slapdash approach might save you time in the short term, you won't attain a high success rate, and therefore, ultimately you'll waste time. It is always worth investing those extra few hours, or days, or weeks, getting the application into the best shape possible before submitting. Give each one its best chance. And, as usual, if at first, you don't succeed, don't give up, just turn your attention to the next one on the list.

Lloyds TSB Foundation https://www.lloydsbankfoundation.org.uk/

Francis W. Reckitt www.reckittarts.org/applications-status/status

Esmee Fairbairn Foundation https://esmeefairbairn.org.uk/what-we-fund/arts

Stage One https://www.stageone.uk.com/

The Andrew Lloyd Webber Foundation https://www.andrewlloydwebberfoundation.com/content/category/grants

The Oxford Samuel Beckett Theatre Trust Award https://www.osbttrust.com/award.html

The National Lottery http://www.lotterygoodcauses.org.uk/funding

The Noel Coward Foundation https://www.noelcoward.org/

Heritage Lottery Fund https://www.heritagefund.org.uk

The Theatres Trust https://www.theatrestrust.org/how-we-help/grants-funding

The Garrick Arts Trust https://www.garrickclub.co.uk/charitable_trust

Suez Trust https://www.suezcommunitiestrust.org.uk/apply-for-funding

The Garfield Weston Foundation https://www.garfieldweston.org

Foyle Foundation https://www.foylefoundation.org.uk/main-grants-scheme-arts/

George Goetchius & Donald Howarth Society of Friends Awards (Write to: G&D SOFAS, 9 Lower Mall, London, W6 9DJ)

Paul Hamlyn Foundation https://www.phf.org.uk/

National Endowment for Science, Technology and the Arts https://www.nesta.org.uk/

Welcome Trust https://www.wellcome.ac.uk/funding

Jerwood Charitable Foundation https://jerwoodarts.org/

The Fenton Arts Trust https://www.fentonartstrust.org.uk

MGC Futures https://www.mgcfutures.com/

A SEED COMMISSION

A seed commission is when a theatre pays a writer to draft a new theatre text. These plays are not meant to be perfect, but a work-in-progress, an early draft that gives an indication of what the completed text might be like. Certainly, they have the potential to become a full commission in time, with work. This type of initiative usually involves a dramaturge or dramaturgical support from the literary manager. There will often be, at the very least, a rehearsed reading of the play at the end of the commission.

The amount paid is not high, perhaps less than £2,000, and there is no obligation for the theatre to take the work beyond the seed commission stage. Some writers have issues with seed commissions. As one playwright said to me, "I feel as if I'm a barman and someone has ordered a pint of Guinness, and I pour it with care and let it settle and then when I go to hand it to the customer, they've skidadled." In order to avoid disappointment, again, do make sure that the writer understands where the seed commission will likely lead, or not. Rebecca Mairs outlines their importance at the Lyric in Belfast:

> Communication with writers is essential. I'm consistently in touch with and having conversations with writers of promise, and I ensure that we abide by the guidelines set down by the Writers Guild of Great Britain. I will also suggest commissions to Jimmy Faye, our artistic director – but that decision ultimately lies with Jimmy. I oversee the talent development programme which has been a great success. In our most recent call out we received 330 submissions, which is up on 72 in our first year. It is a very good way to gauge what is interesting people, and to find out who is writing and who the new voices are.
>
> We will also look at funding seed commissions. I try to be responsive to theatre-makers, and to incorporate all pathways to theatre in our programme, not only single-authored pieces. I might, for example, arrange a session with a choreographer as part of our talent development programme. I understand that people work in different ways. I provide feedback on as much work as I can, as that is a key part of the job. Finding time to read it all can still be a challenge.[5]

Figure 5.8 Actors and Director Jim Nolan at Table Read.

WRITERS RESIDENCIES

Another way a playwright can be supported in writing their play is to spend time at a writers' residency – which the literary manager can either organise or assist the playwright in their application.

Artist residence programmes are opportunities provided by a host organisation that enable a creative person to spend focused time on their art. A residency will give the writer a refuge from the worries and demands of everyday living, allowing the creative mind to concentrate on their project, uninterrupted. The usual deal is that a writer will reside for a time in an alternative environment and work, research, explore and develop new work. Some programmes might also provide food and others, occasionally, a stipend for the duration of the playwright's tenure. A small number of residencies will have specially equipped rooms where theatre-makers can carry out rehearsed readings and workshops and other aspects of the research and development process. It is even possible that you as the literary manager or dramaturg could join the playwright at some point to provide some dramaturgical workshops and early feedback. It all depends on the requirements of the individual residency, the needs of the playwright, and what funding is available to you for this project. A residency is a great resource for a playwright working on a new play. As a literary manager you should have a working knowledge of all these residencies, and if at all possible, you should actively cultivate a mutually beneficial relationship between your theatre and one or two specific programmes.

Figure 5.9 Writer's Bedroom at the Tyrone Guthrie Centre, Ireland.

The tradition of artist-in-residency programmes began, in its modern sense, over a hundred years ago in the USA when the Yaddo Residency was launched, in 1900, with a mission "to nurture the creative process by providing an opportunity for artists to work without interruption in a supportive environment."[6] The best, most prestigious, and most generous of these institutions are still found in North America. Residencies were slowly established elsewhere around the world, mostly from the mid-20th century onwards. Today, you'll find them in every country. They are places that provide time and space for workers from within the creative arts: visual artists, writers, musicians, dancers, and film makers – allowing them to ring-fence focused time to complete a project, or an aspect of a project. Here, the writer can leave aside everyday responsibilities and worries, spend time on their art, reflecting, researching and producing in a unique, inspiring environment.

Figure 5.10 Tyn-y-Pant, Writers' Residency Powys, Wales.

As a literary manager, writers' residencies are very useful when offering a development programme at your theatre, a particularly attractive resource when a mentored playwright is working on a specific project. If, say, you have a writer on attachment at your theatre for a year, and during this time you have agreed that they will write a new play, you might offer that they spend a period at a residency writing up the initial draft. The playwright may even be able to return to the same, or another, residency for revisions following workshops and feedback. The duration of the residency will depend on many factors, not least of which is how much time the playwright can realistically step away from real life, how much time is offered by the residency, and how much funding you can obtain to facilitate all of this.

Offering such an initiative will ensure your theatre is all the more attractive for emerging talent. A literary manager is therefore well-advised to establish a partnership with a residency programme. Also, occasionally a theatre might want to consider hosting a theatre artist itself – but does not have the physical space to do so. Perhaps, for example, your theatre is interested in working with a playwright who writes in another language and lives in another country, and/or whose approach or use of form is an aspect your theatre wishes to explore, and you wish to invite them to your theatre for a period to support them in their art, and to learn from them. In this instance, a partnership with an established residency can be all the more useful for your theatre as they might host the playwright for you. Not all residencies are advertised, many rely on word-of-mouth. They do not have to be located in historic houses in rural idylls beyond the beyond, they can just as easily be in the city centre. A literary manager would do very well to get to know what residency programmes are available in their neighbourhood, and if they aren't to be found, don't rule out approaching institutions such as local universities to see if you can set one up in partnership with your theatre. Universities should be able to provide accommodation, particularly in the summer months, and in exchange you can perhaps offer the educational establishment a lecture/workshop on playwriting or dramaturgy, by either yourself and/or the visiting playwright. Such initiatives have reputational value for universities and many will be open to discussing the possibility with you. You might also approach the third party for funding to provide a stipend for the visiting writer.

What is involved in a residency depends entirely on the specific programme. Some residencies require a level of interactivity with a local community, which may include giving writing workshops or performing a play-reading, or presenting at the local school, for example. Others might place importance on some artistic discourse and engagement with the immediate environment, or the history and traditions of the location, or creating a piece of theatre inspired by the locale.

If there are other writers and artists at the residency, a cross-pollination of ideas and a creative discussion is usually encouraged. These conversations will normally take place over dinner or via readings, studio tours, and talks. In many ways, the artists' residency deliberately mirrors the meeting places of the great art movements – think of Les Deux Magots in Paris, or Greenwich Village's Café Wha in their heyday – a residency is an environment that promotes the meeting of creative minds and the progression, debate, and discussion of ideas. Obviously, such a scenario will also

Figure 5.11 A Lighthouse and Donkey on Inis Oírr, Aran Islands, Co. Galway, Ireland, Where the Áras Éanna Residency Is located.

provide ample opportunity for artists to network. In this way, a playwright who is of a sociable bent is possibly going to benefit most. It's nonetheless always important that your playwright is respectful of boundaries, and the work needs of other artists in residence.

In contrast, some residencies involve complete isolation. If this is the case, you must ensure that your playwright is psychologically fit to handle isolation, is resourceful enough to navigate any practical issues that may arise, and is comfortable with their own company for an extended period. What all residencies will want is for your writer to prioritise their work and to take the residency seriously.

As to what is provided, it really depends on the residency. The label 'residency' denotes that the place has some sort of charitable status and is not being run as a business. Accommodation is often free, or when it isn't, it's heavily subsidised so it's affordable. Some residencies provide food. Some provide a stipend. Some provide both, some neither. Most are situated in a location of note, it might be a very beautiful place, or an interesting building, or historically important, or quirky. You will have to give consideration and research each one to see which best suit your requirements.

As mentioned above, the US boasts the three most prestigious and longest established residencies: Yaddo, McDowell, and Millay. Attending any in this trinity anoints immediate status on the playwright, and it's a coveted career high just to be accepted. At these institutions, the playwright would be provided with room and board, perhaps a stipend also, and a beautiful environment in which to work. They are likely to meet a great many other creative people there, and some may be household

Figure 5.12 Near Heinrich Boell's Writers' Residency, Achill, Ireland.

names. The concentration of creative minds is inspiring and often results in fruitful collaborations and can provide excellent networking opportunities. Obviously, a stay at any of these institutions is much sought after and the competition for places is stiff. The playwright would have to have an impressive CV and track record to even be considered for these top residencies. However, if your theatre has standing in the international theatre community and you are supporting their application, it will help with their application.

Applications to residencies can be time-consuming and the emerging playwright will likely need help in this process, or you may be able to apply on their behalf and offer the residency as part of a developmental package from your theatre. Residencies are institutions to which the playwright must apply and demonstrate their professionalism as a playwright, perhaps via a portfolio, reviews, publications and references, and a CV/resume that shows they are considered by their peers to be a practicing professional artist.

Figure 5.13 The Tyrone Guthrie Centre, Ireland.

Not all residencies are free, some charge a fee, but they are usually subsidised by a local authority, private foundation, or charitable trust, so, such the fee is normally manageable – and much less than a stay at an equivalent building that is run as a hotel. For writers on this side of the pond, it's truly Murphy's law that most of the residencies offering entirely free accommodation are in the USA, which of course means that there's still a hefty airfare to pay and that rather negates the free accommodation. Still, the Arts Council and charities, such as Francis W. Reckitt and Peggy Ramsay, are open to applications for assistance in covering the cost of a residential stay and this covers airfares.

There are a great number of respected residencies which are less well-known, where entry is less competitive and the requirements less strict – so don't limit your search to the better-known residencies. Sometimes residencies can also offer courses – the UK's Arvon Foundation is a good example of this kind, where playwrights can spend a week being tutored by key industry figures.

Should you want to establish a relationship between your theatre and an established arts residency, you might chance partnering with an establishment that doesn't receive a great volume of applications, perhaps a newly opened residency, or one in an off-the-beaten-path location.

Possibly consider a retreat.[7] They differ from residencies in that they provide a similar service, but for a hotel-standard fee – which can be high. Retreats are not usually subsidised by national, private, or corporate funding and don't have normally have charitable status. Retreats are often run as a business, usually by artists or art lovers. If you manage to secure funding, however, then retreats are just as good – and

Figure 5.14 The Hurst Arvon Centre, Shropshire, England.

sometimes even better than residencies. As retreats are keen to attract guests, there is rarely any application process beyond a booking. If a process exists, it is unlikely to be juried or terribly rigorous. For this reason, a retreat might be a solution for an early career playwright, if you can secure funding to cover costs. Bear in mind that retreats tend not to bestow the prestige associated with a subsidised residency.

As a literary manager, it really is a good idea to spend time researching and familiarising yourself with residencies and retreats you feel resonate with the spirit of your theatre. Compile a shortlist of those that offer the type of residency you feel would suit your playwrights best. Some residencies might favour the visual arts, others music, others dance – but all will accept an application from a writer. There are residencies with a particular connection with the theatre arts, such as Tyn-y-Pant in Wales, the Albee Foundation in Montauk, New York, and the Tyrone Guthrie Centre in Co. Monaghan, Ireland – and these may be good starting points for a theatre's literary manager looking to forge relationships with residencies. It is useful to have a phone or Zoom conversation with the director of a residency programme, in the first instance. A residency may state on their website that they cater only for visual artists for example, but an enquiry could reveal that you're in luck, that they'd be delighted to partner with a theatre and have been considering doing so for a while. They may also let you know of a bursary or other source of funding, which has not been advertised and of which you might avail. Equally, they may tell you that they're concentrating on poets for the foreseeable and an application from a theatre/theatre artist won't make it past the jury. Knowing this fact will save you time. So, do make sure you directly approach the residencies on your short-list and book that initial conversation.

Figure 5.15 Ginistrelle Artists' Centre, Assissi, Italy.

What is usually needed for this environment to work well for your playwright, is for them to have a plan and goal in hand before they arrive. The playwright can deviate from the plan, of course, but a framework helps to keep the paralysis of disorientation at bay. Indeed, as part of the application process, the playwright will normally have to state what they hope to achieve whilst on residency. This itemisation can provide a good opportunity for you and the playwright to thrash out and write down what you both think they might attain within this time. There is no blueprint, obviously. It will depend on where in the process the playwright is, how long they'll be in-residence, and how they personally work, and their pace and creative approach.

EARLY STAGES

If at the very beginning of a project, the playwright might want to spend time reading and researching, walking and thinking, and eventually drawing up an overview or treatment and perhaps some sample scenes or dialogue exchanges to get a flavour of the piece nailed. In this case, you might quantify how time will be spent with numbers (application procedures love quantitative detail). For example, you could propose that in the two weeks at the institution, your playwright will aim to research material for the play by reading four relevant texts, reviewing six relevant interviews and drawing up a two-page plan for the proposed structure of the play, a character breakdown, and will write five sample pages of script to set down the tone and voice for the piece. Make sure both you and the playwright are in agreement on what can be realistically achieved in the time frame.

MID STAGE

At this point, your playwright has likely carried out all the research necessary, has notes and samples of dialogue, a few draft scenes, has made decisions on structure, the characters are sketched out and developed – what they have to do now is sit down and write. This is a good time to head off to a residency, but a plan is still needed. Whilst it might sound more corporate than theatre, meeting with the playwright and asking them to set out some SMART goals is helpful. The SMART framework gives tractability to their objectives and provides verifiable trajectories towards their ultimate goal, identifying milestones along the way and measuring the attainability of the playwright's aim. Make sure goals are realistic. The chart below is merely a suggestion and will be too prescriptive for some, but it will be very useful for others.

> Specific – What does the playwright want to achieve? A 70-page first draft of the play?
>
> Measurable – Include milestones, how many acts, scenes? Agree roughly on page count.
>
> Attainable – Be realistic. Can this be done? In a week unlikely. In two months, a draft, yes.
>
> Relevant – Is the activity they are planning for their time there relevant to the project?
>
> Timely – Pace. Perhaps set a 2-page goal per day. Agree on how many want at deadline.

END STAGE

At this point in the process, the playwright will be looking for time to revise, rewrite, edit, hone and polish the work ready for submission/rehearsals. It will likely come after some workshops, perhaps a rehearsed reading, and definitely some dramaturgical notes from you or another dramaturge. At this point, you will meet with the writer to make sure that they have fully understood and processed any dramaturgical notes they've received. Discuss how they feel about questions raised. Ask where they agree with suggestions, where they don't, and what alternative solutions they might have for issues that have arisen. Once more, help them set out a clear plan of attack, possibly using the SMART approach. It's a balance between not wanting to dictate to the playwright, but providing a structure within which, they can create and revise more effectively. The playwright might enlist the help of fellow residents to do some readings. It might be an idea to schedule a Zoom call with the playwright (if there's wifi!) at a halfway point, to check in and see if they need to discuss issues or if any further questions have arisen.

A common question is whether or not the playwright can simply do all of this at home. Of course, it's not where the playwright writes that matters, but the fact that the playwright does so in a regular and focused manner. A playwright can undoubtedly spend a year on a prestigious writers' colony and come up with nothing but a few shoddy

Figure 5.16 The Tyrone Guthrie Centre, Ireland.

scenes of self-indulgent nonsense. And, the seminal play of our times could absolutely be written in a cramped city-centre apartment full of screaming kids and surrounded by noisy neighbours. This scenario is possible, but it is not easy, or even likely. Time and seclusion from everyday worries and responsibilities in an attractive environment undoubtedly help and facilitate the creative process, and it is your job as a literary manager to ensure that the playwright is given the best environment to reach their full potential. Attending an artists' residency will focus the playwright's mind and encourage their productivity. Furthermore, for the emerging writer, a residency is an affirmation that they are a serious and professional playwright and are considered so by their peers, which aids their confidence and in turn, helps them to take their own work seriously.

For many, an added benefit of a residency is the conversations to be had with other artists. During the daytime, artists are busy at work. In the evenings, however, they will frequently make their own events or happenings, reading work to one another and getting feedback, showing their visual art, playing music, singing, listening to critiques, and discussing all aspects of their projects – this is invaluable for the playwright hoping to grow in their profession. Visiting a residency in another country and culture can be an education in itself. Writers might be enticed to combine the use of residencies with an opportunity to feed their work with global experiences.

Figure 5.17 The Tumbleweed Residency, Shakespeare and Company, Left Bank, Paris.

Not all residencies are communal. Some have an emphasis on the isolation of course, a set-up that will suit some writers more than others. The Áras Éanna Residency is an example of this type of establishment.[8] Located on the island of Inis Oírr,[9] the smallest of Ireland's Aran Islands, it is one of Europe's most westerly and remote points. In winter months, it can provide the silence and solitary existence some playwrights might require – and there is a community theatre space in which they may be able to avail. If the playwright doesn't speak Irish, there will be a further layer of isolation added to the experience, and this removal may be additionally beneficial, potentially. Tyn-y-Pant[10] near Builth Wells in Wales is another residency that will allow for splendid isolation. This 400-year-old stone building was the rural retreat of the late playwright, director, and literary manager at the Royal Court Theatre, Donald Howarth. A rustic barn conversion, it is now largely run as a residency for playwrights. It is situated on a wild common in scenic, rural Powys, in the upper part of the Wye valley. Howarth wrote a number of his plays here, and he and his civil partner George Goetchius, are buried in the garden. Tyn-y-Pant is a newly created residency, wonderfully located, full of theatre history, and a very good starting point for a literary manager hoping to make connections with such a charity.

Emerging playwrights often talk about a metamorphosis occurring when on residency. Time spent on retreat enables them to crystallise their thoughts and come to terms with the reality of being a playwright. A good number of emerging playwrights will be travelling over a bridge from another career – and as exciting as this process can be, it is also traumatic. Time spent alone can help with conceptualising and developing their theatre work, their worldview, how they want to approach their art, and also with seeing themselves as professional playwrights. At an arts residency, the playwright can begin to understand how creativity works for them. Here, the pressure of life is off, they are alone and this situation facilitates the percolation of ideas. Thoughts appear, form, and change and move from the back brain to the fore. Some writers will experiment with other art forms when there, and what is gained from these disciplines will inform their own writing practice. A residency permits them to play and to grow.

I've drawn up a list of residencies here. It is by no means exhaustive, there are undoubtedly others, in many more countries. Nonetheless, this list is a good starting point and includes the better-known institutions. It has been complied with a focus on residencies that are open to applications from playwrights (even where there is a greater concentration on anther art form, such as the visual). As always, if you are considering an approach with a view to a partnership with your theatre, do make direct contact with the residency's director in the first instance as this may prove helpful and, at the very least, will alert you if you are wasting your time on an application.

Britain

Residencies:

Gladstone's Library (Flintshire, Wales) http://www.gladstoneslibrary.com

Hawkwood College (Gloucestershire, England) http://www.hawkwoodcollege.co.uk

Hawthornden Castle (Midlothian, Scotland) http://www.hawthorndenliteraryretreat.org

Hospitalfield (Arbroath, Scotland) http://www.hopitalfield.org.uk

Cove Park (Argyll and Bute, Scotland) http://covepark.org/residencies-overview

Arvon Foundation (Shropshire, Devon, Lancashire, Inverness) http://www.arvon.org

Retreats:

Urban Writers' http://urbanwritersretreat.co.uk

Ireland

Residencies:

Áras Éanna (Aran Islands, Co. Galway) http://aras-eanna.ie/en/residencies/

Tyrone Guthrie Centre (Co. Monaghan) http://www.tyroneguthrie.ie/

Heinrich Boell's Cottage (Achill Island, Co. Mayo) http://heinrichboelcottage.com

Cill Rialaig (Co. Kerry) cillrialaigartscentre.com/residencies/

Dublin Writer in Residence http://www.dcu.ie/english/2021/sep/writer-residence

Retreats:

The River Mill (Co. Down) http://www.the-river-mill.co.uk
Anam cara (Co. Cork) http://www.anamcararetreat.com
Molly Keane Writers Retreat (Co. Waterford) http://www.themollykeanehouse.com

Continental Europe

France
Residencies:

Chateau la Napoule (Cannes) http://www.chateau-lanapoule.com/en/
Centre Culturel Irlandais (Paris) http://www.centreculturelirlandais.com/en/
Shakespeare and Company (Paris) http://shakespeareandcompany.com/35/history/38/about-tumbleweeds
Dora Maar House (Menerbes) https://core.slideroom.com/#/Login
Retreats:
La Muse Inn (High Pyrenees) http://www.lamuseretreat.com

Monaco
The Ireland Funds Monaco http://Irelandfunds.org/chapters/worldwide/Monaco/bursaries
Germany
Schwarndorf http://www.kebbelvilla.de/en/international-artist-residence-program

Italy
Bogliasco Foundation (Liguria) https://www.bfny.org
Ginestrelle (Umbria) http://www.artestudioginestrelle.wordpress.com
Santa Maddelena Foundation (Tuscany) http://www.santamaddelena.org/fellowships
Siena http://www.sienaart.org/residencies/summer-residency-program/summer-residency-description/

USA

Residencies:
Adirondack (New York State) https://adirondackcenterforwriting.org/residency/

Albee Foundation (Long Island, New York) https://www.albeefoundation.org/
Anderson Centre (Minnesota) https://www.andersoncenter.org/
Art Croft (Kentucky) https://artcroft.org/residents
Atlantic Centre (Florida) https://atlanticcenterforthearts.org/
Caldera Arts (Oregon) https://www.calderaarts.org/ourprograms
Djerassi (California) https://djerassi.org/
Dorland (California) https://www.dorlandartscolony.com
Exeter (New Hampshire) http://www.exeter.edu/about-us/career-opportunities/fellowships/george-bennett-fellowship
Hambidge (Georgia) https://www.hambidge.org/
Headlands (California) https://www.headlands.org/
Hedgebrook (Washington State) https://www.hedgebrook.org/
Hugo House (Seattle) https://hugohouse.org/upcoming-events/hugohouse-fellowship/
Jentle (Wyoming) http://jentelarts.org/
Kerouac (Florida) https://www.kerouacproject.org/
KFW (Kentucky) https://www.kfw.org/retreats-residencies/
Kulcher (Minnesota) https://www.kulcher.org/programs/artist-retreat/
Kimmel (Nebraska) https://www.khncenterforthearts.org/
Lynchburg (Virginia) https://www.lynchburg.edu/academics/majors-and-minors/english/thornton/
Montalvo Arts (California) https://www.montalvoarts.org/experience/lucas-artists-residency-program/programs/
Mastheads (Massachusetts) https://www.themastheads.org/residency
Macdowell (New Hampshire) https://www.macdowell.org/
Millay (New York State) https://www.macdowell.org/
Norton Island (Maine) https://www.esasternfrontier.org/
OMI (New York) https://www.artomi.org/
Spring creek (Oregon) https://www.macdowell.org/
Radcliffe (Massachusetts) https://www.radcliffe.harvard.edu/radcliffe-fellowship
Rocky Mountain (Colorado) https://www.nps.gov/romo/getinvolved/supportyourpark/artist_in_residence.htm
Studio in the Woods (New Orleans) https://www.astudiointhewoods.org/series/artistic/
Saltonstall (New York State) https://www.saltonstall.org/residencies/juried-residencies/
Virginia Centre (Virginia) https://www.vcca.com/
Ucross (Wyoming) https://www.ucrossfoundation.org/residency-program.html
Vermont Studio (Vermont) https://vermontstudiocenter.org/
Wild Acres (North Carolina) https://wildacres.org/events/?category=writers-storytellers

Wellstone Center (California) http://www.wellstoneredwoods.org/wcr-writing-fellowship/
Woodstock (New York) https://www.woodstockguild.org/artist-residencies/
Wurlitzer (New Mexico) https://wurlitzerfoundation.org/
Write On (Wisconsin) http://writeondoorcounty.org/residency/
Yaddo (New York state) https://www.yaddo.org/
Vinyards (various, USA and Canada) http://www.writingbetweenthevines.org

Canada

Banff https://www.banffcentre.ca/programs
Saskatchewan https://skwriter.com/retreats/writer-and-artist-retreats
Joy Kogawa House (Vancouver) https://www.kogawahouse.com/wp/residencies/

Australia

Varuna https://www.varuna.com.au/residencies

LIFE ADVICE

A literary manager is neither a real estate agent nor a recruitment specialist however, these are probably the two areas where early career playwrights struggle most, outside of writing. At some point, every writer you mentor is going to ask you for advice either on earning money or finding accommodation:

ADVISING WRITERS ON EMPLOYMENT

A wise writer once said to me that it's not so much the pram in the hall that's the impediment to a writing career, but the bills on the door-mat. Money worries are the bane of creativity. And unless independently wealthy, the emerging playwright will have to make a living while waiting for that West End hit (and probably for a while after that fact too). It's a common dilemma for writers and they'll often seek advice on this topic from a literary manager. Perhaps advise them to consider the following:

Journalism is an obvious choice and is still, probably, the most common second career for many creative writers. A journalistic background provides marvellous training re-editing and brevity of approach. Copy-writing, particularly website copy, is also a popular income booster for the writer but both copy-writing and journalism are less satisfying forms of writing for the creative writer and spending all day writing on the day job can make it difficult to come home and do the same at night.

Teaching English and/or creative writing is another common earner for writers. TEFL training and experience has the advantage of lending a writer a sound understanding of grammar and the intricacies of the English language – all of which are of great practical and transferrable use. A TEFL teacher also (usually) travels and such experiences can feed into the writer's work. Teaching creative writing allows the writer to deconstruct the tools of creative writing, which may benefit their own writing. However, the writer will usually need a track record of publication/staged productions before getting work in this area.

It is not uncommon for writers to work a mundane job such as on a factory line or as a manual labourer. Such tasks sit quite well with a writing career as they give the writer time to think, to let ideas bubble and boil ready to write down after the shift has finished. Also, with a job so utterly removed from writing, the writer will be fresh and eager to sit at your laptop of an evening. More pertinently, the writer gets to experience real life up close. Think of the playwright and TV writer Nell Dunn, a young woman from an upper-middle-class background whose day-job in a Battersea sweet factory provided the 1960s inspired the TV classic *Up The Junction*. The downside of any brain numbing, repetitive work is that it has no status. This fact should not be important but it is because writers are human, so for a writer to stay in a lowly job, s/he needs determination, focus, and confidence in their reason for doing this type of work.

Writers, of course, come from all walks of life and all career backgrounds. For writers who may be considering giving up their job to write full time, you may need to remind that (most likely) they'll still need to make a living. Maybe the job they have is not glamorous or interesting, but these are often the best complementary jobs for writing. So, if they really want to be a writer, the greatest sacrifice they make may be NOT giving up the day job – but rather, staying with it.

ADVISING WRITERS ON ACCOMMODATION

When researching my Ph.D. I had to move to London, a city with eye-wateringly high rents. Faced with no income, accommodation was quite a dilemma in those circumstances. However, I discovered, and opted for an alternative living situation, sharing with a nonagenarian for peppercorn rent. The gentleman in question lived in a mansion apartment in Kensington, very close to the theatre which was the subject of my research. His home was enormous and there was more than enough room for us both. His medical needs were taken care of by a team of professionals who came by on rota during the week. I was simply a company for him; watching TV together, eating meals together, discussing books, history, and politics. He was a genuinely lovely man and we became friends despite the enormous age difference. I shared his home for some five years, which allowed me to become acquainted with life in Central London and gave me time to look for work, and save up to eventually get my own place. Sadly, this sweet man passed away aged 98, but I'll always be grateful for what that arrangement provided for me – and more pertinently, for the gift of his friendship.

This living arrangement was overseen by an organisation that specialises in cross-generational home-sharing: shareandcare.co.uk. To this day, I recommend it to all writers in need of cheaper accommodation in London.

A writer might also consider joining an organisation that specialises in property guardianship – an arrangement by which tenants are provided with accommodation at a discounted rate, in return for flexibility. Guardianship properties are frequently in desirable locations and are interesting or unusual properties, such as historical buildings or commercial premises. The property owners may be, for example, waiting on planning permission to develop the premises and don't want them left vacant in the interim, and guardians help keep squatters at bay. There is little security in this arrangement, tenants may have to vacate a property with just a couple of weeks' notice, but it may be a very good temporary set-up for a writer struggling to pay rent in an expensive city. Be aware that such an arrangement might involve multiple occupants in a large single property.

Similarly, a writer might keep an ear out for house-sitting arrangements or sublets, which may be advertised on social media, but are more likely to emerge via word-of-mouth/your social network. It's best to let people know you're always interested in these opportunities for writers.

A wise literary manager will only recommend writers for any of the above if fully confident the writer will respect the property and any other persons involved in the arrangement, and that they will fulfil their duties.

NOTES

1. Sue Healy's interview with Simon Stephens, Brick Lane, London, August 13, 2021.
2. Sue Healy's interview with Simon Stephens, Brick Lane, London, August 13, 2021.
3. Sue Healy's interview with Simon Farquhar, Richmond, London, September 16, 2021.
4. Sue Healy's interview with Simon Stephens, Brick Lane, London, August 13, 2021.

5 Sue Healy's interview with Rebecca Mairs, via Zoom, August 10, 2021.
6 http://www.yaddo.org.
7 Confusingly, some subsidised residencies are called retreats, and vice versa. This guide concentrates on establishments that meet the definition of a 'residency,' and specifies where an institution is regarded as a commercial retreat.
8 http://www.aras-eanna.ie/en/residencies
9 Inis Oirr is a *Gaeltacht*, which means that Irish is the first language on the island, though most residents are also fluent in English. Beyond the island of Ireland, the Irish language is sometimes referred to as 'Gaelic' – but this term is confusing as lexically, it also refers to the separate native languages of Scotland and the Isle of Man, which are not spoken in Ireland. The Irish use the term 'Irish' for their native language.
10 Tyn-y-Pant does not yet have a web presence. The residency is administered by the George Goetchius and Donald Howarth Society of Friends Award. For more information and/or to apply, write to: G&D SOFAS Trustees, 9 Lower Mall, Hammersmith, London W6 9DJ. Note that this charity has other properties central to theatre history, in London and Hampshire, which may be made available for residencies in the future.

CHAPTER 6

Diversity and inclusion

UNDERSTANDING YOUR THEATRE'S CULTURE

When you enter an established theatre as the literary manager, you enter a specific culture, you encounter a world with idiosyncratic traditions and peculiar customs, with its own history and way of doing things. George Devine famously said that one should choose one's theatre as one would choose one's religion.[1]

Often, it is difficult for the newly arrived literary manager to navigate the invisible rules and baffling systems and hierarchies that a theatre can present, just as it might be if you were negotiating a new faith. Although you might wish to be the new broom and dismantle all structures and approaches that appear a nonsense to you, it is possibly a good idea to exercise some caution. Take time to study the lie of the land and read as much as you can on the history of the institution. Get to know the backgrounds of your colleagues and gauge if there are patterns. Try to get a sense of why things operate as they do, who really holds the power, what apprehensions exist, who will seem an outsider to them, and why they may fear them. When you want to introduce change, do so as diplomatically as you can, well-informed and mindful of these anxieties. Present the need for change, well backed up with proof of that need. A theatre has a special place in the minds of those who support it, within its community and as progressive as they might want to consider themselves, they'll need convincing that things are really broken before they'll be happy with you fixing it. People are often fiercely loyal to their chosen theatre, tread carefully. You can influence and change how a theatre operates, but this will not happen over-night.

Figure 6.1 Harriet Devine, Former Literary Manager and Daughter of George Devine Co-founder of The English Stage Company at the Royal Court Theatre, Outside Their Former Family Home, 9 Lower Mall London.

INSTITUTIONAL HABITUS

To understand how a theatre and its culture are viewed in the minds of those who support it and those who have supported it, or worked within its structures for a long time, the theory of 'habitus' by the French philosopher Pierre Bourdieu is a helpful lens, particularly the Bourdieu-inspired notion of 'institutional habitus.' Viewing a theatre's power structure through this framework can explain some of the defensiveness one might encounter if wishing to review processes at work, and why it's advisable to progress with caution. It is also useful to refer to habitus if there are problematic areas you have difficulty in getting others to address, or are particularly perplexed as to why others cannot see the issue at hand. This apparently strange unwillingness to deal with the obvious is all likely down to very deep-rooted learned subconscious behaviour – which takes time to address and bring to conscious attention.

Figure 6.2 Statue of Joan Littlewood Outside the Theatre Royal Stratford East, London.

Some scholars have expressed reservations about using the concept of institutional habitus, due to its potential to overstretch and reduce the explanatory power of Bourdieu's theories, particularly in the field of research in education. Institutional habitus is, nonetheless, useful in determining and understanding how far surface events are generated from structures and rules of practice that lie beneath. Bourdieu coined the term 'habitus' from the 'habitual,' or that which is done on a recurrent basis to the point that it becomes quotidian, a habit, an action rendered largely unquestioned and widely accepted as 'how things are.' According to this theory, habitus is a complex structure built of a person's history and reinforced by repeated or habitual actions. Bourdieu proposed that one's social environment, formative experiences, gender, ethnicity, class, and religious background provide structures which in turn prompt a specific way of interpreting the world and guide one's opinions and expectations. Bourdieu's theory helps to comprehend how an individual internalises the external. If an individual has been raised within a governing and privileged class, say, the individual will have a specific way of viewing the world that is distinct from someone who was raised as part of a minority group within the same society. Habitus in this sense will refer to what an individual may take for granted, or what they may understand as 'common sense.' It will inform the vocabulary an individual acquires, how they interact, their judgement, how they develop, their ambitions, and what their expectations are. Habitus is not fixed and the individual is not dominated by their habitus and can contribute to and influence it. Nor is one's habitus exclusively divided along class, generational or ethnic lines, although these factors can influence habitus. Using Bourdieu's theory, power can be seen as a culturally crafted force, bolstered jointly by agency and structure. Habitus, in this view, is neither a result of free will nor is it wholly determined by structures. Rather, it is created by a level of engagement between the two over time – which ultimately leads to leanings, tastes, and opinions that are informed by past events *and* which shape current practices and, crucially, condition our perceptions of these (Bourdieu 1984, p. 170). A person's individual history is constitutive of their habitus, but the concept has also been applied to a collective history, for example, that of an institution. This institutional habitus leads to a distinctive, collective outlook, and informs how constituent members of an institution interact, view each other, and understand and interpret the world around them. Viewed through the lens of institutional habitus, it is possible to understand how the expectations and dispositions of groups and the structure and dynamics of their practices are formed and defined by the forces operating within their own particular social sphere. Often unwittingly, people of a shared habitus will gravitate towards one another and create invisible boundaries between their own and other collectives. Over time, distinctions will be continuously re-enforced and their tastes and opinions become the standard within an institution. The scope and limits of this habitus remain unseen, unconsidered, and unquestioned. Therefore, put simply, your theatre will have its own habitus. Do what you can to understand it, before thinking of how you can address it and the ways in which you can encourage people to shift their thinking.

Whilst it could be argued that Bourdieu's concept of habitus has much in common with the general concept of 'culture.' It is the unwitting, subconscious element that is important here. Those who are connected with your theatre are not wholly aware of its institutional habitus, in the way they would be if it were simply the culture of the theatre. With habitus, there is more emphasis on how our basic understanding, perception, and interpretation of our world is influenced by the complex set of social structures within which we live, to the point that it is largely subconscious and is not driven by agency alone. Crucially, Bourdieu poses that habitus is created through a social, rather than individual, process and it is this aspect that leads to patterns that are not only enduring and transferrable from one context to another, but that can also shift in relation to specific contexts and over time, as society evolves. Therefore, with this theory, Bourdieu presents power as forged by culture and upheld by structure and agency. It should be pointed out that this significant subconscious element to habitus has been criticised as it appears to exonerate the individual. It is precisely this unconscious aspect that is useful for this guide, however, as we are not placing blame here but rather attempting to understand how a theatre might operate, and

Figure 6.3 Gielgud Theatre, Shaftesbury Ave., London.

what unseen forces might steer decisions. As an outsider, the literary manager may be able to see power structures and behaviours that a constituent member of the culture at the theatre would find difficult to perceive. It will serve you well to remember this fact, that you are aware of what the constituent members are not, and because of this, change will face challenge and will take more than a memo. They will need to be made aware of their unconscious bias, and accept that new thinking is needed.

Bourdieu describes habitus as:

> Systems of durable, transposable dispositions, structured structures predisposed to function as structuring structures, that is, as principles which generate and organise practices and representations that can be objectively adapted to their outcomes without presupposing a conscious aiming at ends or an express mastery of the operations necessary in order to attain them.
>
> *(Bourdieu, 1990, p. 53)*[2]

Habitus can, and does, change and adapt according to outside influences but it does so gradually and not readily. In essence, it is a worldview and a way of operating and it is not necessarily a conscious perspective. Employing Bourdieu's concept of habitus is helpful in understanding the internal culture of your theatre, and particularly how its 'institutional habitus,' may be steeped in a specific culture, in which most of its participants were raised. Tread cleverly and carefully and be diplomatic. There may be fears provoked by any threat to this habitus or any challenge to power structures at the institution.

BREAKING DOWN BARRIERS

As a literary manager, you are a gatekeeper. You will decide what plays are recommended to the artistic director. You will be consulted regarding programming, perhaps even casting. That is a lot of power. In the past number of years, particularly since the advent of the #MeToo movement and the emergence of Critical Race Theory, there have been great thrusts in theatre to progress plays by previously occluded and marginalised writers, a group which would include women, writers of colour (or writers from the Global Majority), deaf, disabled or neuro-diverse writers, and LGBTQ+ writers. Literary manager at Fishamble, Gavin Kostick, cites diversity and equality as that company's top priority going forwards, but it is not simply tokenism, the work must be good and Fishamble run development workshops to ensure that all are given the opportunity to develop good work:

> We are aiming for 50/50 gender parity in 2021. We are interested in giving a platform to migrant voices. Quality is always at the forefront obviously, definitely more so than quantity – we want good plays. Additionally, we want to know who is writing and where and our initiatives and call-outs are designed to ensure we are alive to what is happening throughout the island [of Ireland].[3]

Equally, in Belfast, Mairs considers inclusion at the Lyric:

> I also look at creative learning, promoting diversity and working with the marginalized, such as young offenders and working within prisons. We try to serve the community where possible.[4]

From gender parity to migrant stories, what would have been highly unusual and controversial even just 20 years ago is commonplace today. Gender fluid and colour blind (or *Bridgerton*) casting is now the norm and is entirely accepted. Nonetheless, it would be wrong to say that there is now access for all and complete parity in platform provision. There is still work to be done.

Most of the challenges lie in the grey areas of unconscious bias, learned behaviour, and institutional habitus. I have never met a literary manager or a dramaturge who openly or even, I believe, consciously holds racist or homophobic or sexist or fascist views, for example, or believes that the stage is the rightful domain of straight white non-disabled men only. Probably without exception in this country, these theatre professionals normally see themselves as liberal and progressive in worldview and believe that they operate according to these philosophies. Nonetheless, an examination of the percentage of programmed plays given over to those from marginalised communities can often reveal hidden bias.

WAKING THE FEMINISTS (WTF) AT THE ABBEY THEATRE

The national theatre of Ireland, the Abbey Theatre, which receives half of the country's public funding for theatre arts, announced its new season in October, 2015. It was a notable year; the programme was titled 'Waking the Nation' to mark the centenary of the 1916 Easter Uprising which had set Ireland on the path to independence.

However, the theatre's centenary programme credited 18 men and only two women in the line-up of writers and directors.

When challenged on this disparity, the retiring artistic director Fiach Mac Conghail, responded rather glibly on Twitter, "…them's the breaks."

Furious responses were posted in response on social media by designer/arts manager Lian Bell, writer Belinda McKeon, and playwright/literary manager Gavin Kostick. The subject gained further traction when international celebrities including Meryl Streep weighed in, in support of protests. Within a fortnight, playwrights, directors, producers, artistic directors, stage managers, designers, actors, and audience members met en masse at the Abbey to discuss systemic gender issues throughout the Irish theatrical industry. This event became the official launch of a push for diversity and inclusion in Irish (and international) theatre: #WakingTheFeminists (WTF). A chastened Mac Conghail later said he deeply regretted the exclusions and said the reaction made him question his own filters and the factors that influence his decisions.

Figure 6.4 The Abbey Theatre, Dublin.

The onus is on the literary manager to examine their theatre's programme for evidence of exclusion and then to highlight the issue, raising it with the artistic director. The quantitative proof is difficult to ignore. Consider how many black or brown writers were programmed in the previous five years; or disabled, or trans, or female. Compare these figures with the percentage of the population and ask yourself if they are being proportionately represented on your stage. This exercise will be instructive and surprising.

CHECK YOUR LENS AND FILTERS

Listed below are other ways a literary manager can ensure they are not just assessing and evaluating plays through a Western dramaturgical lens, or only from the point of view of a non-disabled person:

- Consider your readers – do they all share the same demographic? Can this homogeneity be addressed?

- Give thought to the plays you encourage your readers to study as part of a training process. How many were written by men? By white people? By non-disabled people? Does the answer surprise you? Can you change this situation?

- Reflect on the subject matter explored in the plays. Make a list of how many dwell on issues of race, disability, sexism? Make a list of the other topics. Consider the themes that are relevant to the daily lives of EVERYONE in your community and ask if you are fully serving the community in this regard.

- Examine the same representational issues in regards to the writers you're mentoring, the workshops you are holding.

- Think of the material you are using in your workshops – can you draw from a more diverse pool of work?

- Share your findings with the managerial team. It is hard to argue with numbers, and as stated above, most people working in theatre are not against progress – they simply need help in seeing that it is needed.

- Make a list of the changes you can make to address all the above.

Nickie Miles-Wildin is an artist, a dramaturge, and was previously head of new writing and associate director at Graeae Theatre Company. Disabled and a wheelchair user herself, she is a champion of placing the Deaf, disabled, and neurodivergent story centre stage. Miles-Wildin would like to see a greater understanding of the need for a much greater degree of theatre access for disabled people, in a literal and metaphorical sense, even when theatres are making an apparent effort to support the disabled community. Giving an example of this exclusion: "If there is perhaps one captioned or BSL performance or audio described performance, it is always a single show in a four week run – and that is usually a matinee."

Miles-Wildin points out that wheelchair users are particularly challenged in terms of access to the fringe, which tend to be above-a-pub venues and are therefore very difficult to negotiate using a wheelchair. She posits that such restraints can have a great impact on development opportunities for Deaf, disabled and neurodivergent writers, who will have far fewer opportunities to attend theatres and therefore their exposure to the art is significantly less than their non-disabled counterparts. It also means fewer fringe venues can show work by d/Deaf, disabled and neurodiverse theatre-makers and, therefore these writers, "don't have that all-important chance to fail on the fringe, to learn from feedback, to sharpen their tools and write a good full-length play. It will take them far longer to develop as writers."

Figure 6.5 Nickie Miles-Wildin, Dramaturge.

Miles-Wildin refers to the progression made in recent years with colour-blind casting and plays by women and urges theatres to take more chances on Deaf, disabled and neurodivergent writers. "It can start with literary managers ensuring that Deaf, disabled and neurodiverse writers are part of their writing groups, reading teams and developmental initiatives." She believes the reluctance thus far is attitudinal.

> Theatres worry that a work by a disabled writer won't be well attended. They should take "that risk" and see what happens. Imagine if twenty years ago theatres didn't put on plays by women because it was too risky. Theatres need to take that risk to make sure things change.

Miles-Wildin believes that the non-disabled have a lot to learn and gain from Deaf, disabled and neurodivergent writers, who can be formally playful with structure due to the impact their impairments have on their own lives. A neurodivergent writer might see the architecture of the play differently, or someone with chronic pain will have varying lengths of scenes, or their approach to the hero's journey (which she dislikes) will be different: "Every day is an inciting incident for a disabled person." Miles-Wildin holds that theatre needs to really open stages to disabled artists and hear their stories, their experiences, and that theatre will be all the richer for it.

According to Miles-Wildin, gatekeepers should check their own ableism, interrogate their learned behaviour and that of their reading team and push for proper access and representation on stages, and on the theatre's literary team. She highlights the fact that everyone is pre-disabled, and that at some point in everyone's life, we will lose some physical ability, particularly as we get older: "With an aging population, very soon more than half the population will be over 50, which means there will be more disabled people, theatres must provide for this section of the population." Miles-Wildin says literary departments must be challenged in this regard. "Certainly, we want to be seen as artists, not disabled artists, but it's a question of intersectionality, and disability is the most intersectional area there is. Theatres must put on our work."[5]

> **USEFUL WEBSITES**
>
> http://www.graeae.org
> http://www.boptheatre.co.uk/disabled-playwright-support-programme/
> http://www.royalcourttheatre.com/playwriting/writers-groups/introductory-groups/

NOTES

1. George Devine in a letter to his godchild, Dame Peggy Ashcroft's son. Donald Howarth's private archive, 9 Lower Mall, London.
2. Bourdieu's definition can be informally simplified as the 'structuring structures of the structured structure.'
3. Sue Healy's interview with Gavin Kostick, via Zoom, July 22, 2021.
4. Sue Healy's interview with Rebecca Mairs, via Zoom, August 10, 2021.
5. Sue Healy's interview with Nickie Miles-Wildin, via Zoom, May 5, 2022.

CHAPTER 7

The issue of pay

A CONSIDERATION OF THE CHALLENGES FACING A FRINGE THEATRE: TO PAY OR NOT TO PAY READERS

In Chapter 1, I looked at compensation for the literary manager and the fact that the theatre is generally not a well-paid industry. Literary managers are, on the whole, quite slightly compensated and sometimes we are not compensated at all. Here in this chapter, I am considering payment for the literary team, how to fund a literary department on the fringe, and the ethical questions surrounding this topic. This topic is a matter of much debate in the smaller theatres of Britain and Ireland, a conversation that has played out in intra-industry battles on Twitter on past occasions.

Theatres making a significant profit and/or in receipt of public funding should and usually do allocate a certain amount of their budget for the remuneration of script readers. This fee is not generally high and varies from theatre to theatre, and country to country. As a rough guide, however, per script the fee usually ranges from the price of a sandwich from a corner shop to the price of a lunch in a local café – just as it was at the Royal Court back in the 1960s, as Harriet Devine pointed out in Chapter 1, recalling her time there as a literary manager in the late 1960s. Payment, with inflation considered therefore, has not improved – but script readers do get compensated at funded venues, and funded theatres usually allocate a specific budget to support a reading team.

Many smaller fringe theatres are unfunded, however, and they frequently operate on the thinnest of budgets. For these playhouses, paying for script-readers is difficult, probably not possible at all, and therefore, they rely on volunteerism to process their unsolicited scripts. In exchange for their time, effort, and expertise, these volunteer readers gain experience with an established literary department where they hone their dramaturgical skills and have this internship on their CVs, which will help with job searches within the industry. Obviously, however, this is an ethically ambiguous approach to compensation.

A CASE STUDY

Since 2015, I have served as literary manager at the multi-award-winning Finborough Theatre. This venue is a tiny fringe playhouse, an above-a-pub venue, in London that is broadly considered to "punch above its weight."[1,2] The Finborough has incubated important talent since it was founded in 1980 and has featured prominently in the early careers of major industry figures such as: producer Nica Burns, comedian Jo Brand, actor Rachel Weiss, and directors such as Kate Wasserberg, as well as a host

Figure 7.1 The Finborough Theatre, West Brompton, London.

of playwrights. Our feisty little playhouse aims to champion and foster new writers and revive pre-WWII neglected classics. Very largely unfunded, in order to achieve, maintain and progress these joint objectives, this theatre has had to be innovative and canny in terms of financing projects and has relied heavily on good will and industry willingness to work for a significantly reduced payment, in exchange for experience and/or exposure. There is now a growing and understandable pressure for fair pay for all attached to the theatre, which has been amplified on social media in recent years.

The Finborough's complex relationship with funding provides a good example of the pressures that a fringe theatre will face in terms of financing day-to-day operations. The Finborough is making strides to rectify the payment issue and the artistic director is exploring viable routes to progress. Therefore, the theatre serves as a good case study, or at least a discussion point, for other venues in similar situations.

Seating a maximum audience of 50, the tiny theatre has a surprising history of attracting emerging playwrights of note, such as James Graham, Mark Ravenhill, and Laura Wade, who have progressed to become voices of national and international standing. By providing the first platform for promising playwrights, the theatre's importance within the ecology of contemporary London theatre has frequently and consistently been recognised and lauded by leading industry figures in the UK. It presents plays, old and new, and very occasionally musical theatre and divides the programme between thought-provoking text-based new writing, and the rediscovering of neglected works from the 19th and early 20th centuries. It boasts an impressive track record of accomplishment and achievement, yet The Finborough is not a National Portfolio Organisation (an organisation in receipt of public funding, referred to as an NPO).[3] As such, it has had to operate with little or no funding.

The fact that the theatre plays a key role in the structure of London theatre is broadly agreed. In 2010, referring to the upcoming Finborough's Vibrant Festival featuring new plays to mark its 30th anniversary (among them James Graham's *The Man*), the then *Guardian* theatre critic Lyn Gardner commented: "The Finborough's achievement is a mighty one, doing more for new writing on little or no money than some other, better-funded theaters."[4] Gardner has also subsequently hailed the canny curation of Neil McPherson's artistic directorship, who has been artistic director since 1999.[5] A remarkable proportion of Finborough shows have transferred to the West End and Broadway, or have subsequently toured the Anglophone world: the UK, the USA, Canada, South Africa, Ireland, and Australia. Modern classics that were fostered and received their premiere at The Finborough before achieving significant success and exposure internationally, include Ravenhill's *Shopping and F***king* (1996), Anthony Neilson's *Penetrator* (1993), Laura Wade's *Young Emma* (2003), Martin McDonagh's *The Pillowman* (1995) and Dawn King's *Foxfinder* (2012). It is a track record of disproportionate and significant success for a small fringe venue that is not in receipt of any public funding.

McPherson's determination to maintain standards and foster bold, often provoking, truant and oppositional theatre – a luxury normally the reserve of publicly funded theatres in London such as the Royal National Theatre or the Royal Court Theatre – is one of the main reasons The Finborough is held in high regard by critics

Figure 7.2 *Imaginationship* (dir. Tricia Thorns), Atilla Akinci and John Sackville at The Finborough.

and playwrights alike. Funded venues can financially afford a 'right to fail'[6] policy, for a percentage of their productions at least. It's significant that The Finborough holds its own within this territory, occasionally eschewing a need for financial success in pursuit of advancing an artistic journey. This approach, however, difficult it can be, is fruitful. The theatre's reputation ensures it attracts leading critics to its shows, and for this reason, almost every production staged at The Finborough is reviewed in the UK's national press. Additionally, possibly a direct result of the press attention a billing at The Finborough can provide, The Finborough has been notably successful in wooing significant emerging talent.

The Finborough's running costs are steep, however, the services it needs to finance to run day-to-day operations are expensive. Additionally, the venue is situated within the comfortable environs of London's West bordering the even more affluent Chelsea and Earls Court. Accordingly, the theatre pays annual rent of £38,000. These expenses must be met before any thought is given to funding a production or hiring and paying staff.

Operating within such a restrictive budget is the greatest challenge the venue faces, and it has always been thus. As a consequence, The Finborough has relied somewhat good will in the form of writers', actors', and directors' willingness to work for modest compensation in return for having their work showcased at such a prestigious venue, particularly with its accompanying near-guarantee of national press attention. Across the theatrical arts there is an affection for this playhouse, and also a respect and awareness that it can deliver the sort of exposure it would be difficult to attract elsewhere on the fringe. For this reason, there is no shortage of talent willing to provide The Finborough with their services, for poor or no monetary compensation.[7]

Figure 7.3 *Imaginationship* (dir. Tricia Thorns), Joanna Bending, Rupert Wickham at The Finborough.

An exposure-as-payment approach is understandably perceived in some quarters as, at best, an ethically questionable method of payment. More generally in the industry, the practice has prompted campaigns such as Equity's own "Professionally Made, Professionally Paid"[8] which seeks fair terms and conditions for emerging performers and encourages the use of the Equity Fringe Agreement.[9] There is now a growing pressure on The Finborough to pay professionals properly and in full. In recent years, such demands have been amplified on social media.

In the interests of full disclosure, I must make it clear that my position as literary manager at The Finborough, remains unpaid.[10] I was aware upon joining the venue's team seven years ago that the theatre did not have the funds to pay me, I wasn't expecting payment, and the matter was not discussed further. I viewed the arrangement as an internship as I sought to learn about the inner workings of a London theatre, improve my knowledge of dramaturgy, and the structures of a literary department, and to make contacts in the broader industry. I no longer need to build networks, at least not to a great extent. My PhD has led to a permanent position in academia where I am respectably compensated, and as a playwright I've had a number of plays staged/broadcast and screenplays optioned, so my standing in the creative community is established to some degree. Nonetheless, I remain at the Finborough because I find the work interesting and rewarding and I support what the theatre does. I've become increasingly aware of criticism of the theatre's poor compensation record, however, and am now keen to explore what possible paths forward there are, and how I might play a role in addressing this from the standpoint of a literary manager.

Firstly, it is important to explicitly state that the artistic director does wish to pay staff and to see that the cast and crew are properly compensated. The theatre has very

Figure 7.4 A Fringe Venue, London.

recently employed two fully paid employees for its office. Moreover, the theatre now strives to ensure that productions provide payment for performers. The advent of the Fringe Agreement has helped move the situation in the right direction and as a result the Finborough now includes clauses in its production contracts that adhere with directions outlined by the agreement.[11]

The fringe has been slower to sign up for Equity agreements because things have always been done differently on these edges of the theatre scene. Up until the 1980s and the arrival of Thatcher, profit share and pots of funding with very few strings attached were the fringe norm. Whilst funding is still available, it now comes with increased restrictions, provisos, caveats, and issues that are well meaning, and in many cases admirable and to be encouraged, but they are designed for the West End and West End profits and budgets. They don't transfer very well into the ecology of the fringe. The Finborough is largely a receiving house, with considerable overheads, and expensive rates to pay. Although it offers one of the lowest rental rates on the fringe, the theatre is financially obliged to charge rent. Mounting an average production at The Finborough will typically cost between £30,000 and £40,000 to stage. With 50 seats and tickets selling for £18 per head, it is almost impossible to generate profit. The reality is that if all were paid, there'd be far fewer plays on the fringe, and far fewer venues to present them.

The Finborough hasn't been entirely unfunded, the theatre has obtained small and limited amounts over the years, though it would never have been catagorised as an NPO. The theatre was granted government aid in the fall of 2020, to help ensure its survival into the post-pandemic era. On October 12, 2020, the UK's then Culture Secretary Oliver Dowden announced a Culture Recovery Fund package designed

Figure 7.5 Fringe Fun.

Figure 7.6 Fringe Fun; Handing Out Flyers at the Edinburgh Fringe.

to secure venues during this time of mass closures due to the restrictions placed on entertainment venues due to the pandemic. The Finborough Theatre successfully applied for and was granted £59,574 from the Department for Digital, Culture, Media and Sport (DCMS). The grant ensured that the venue reopened and resumed live performances in the aftermath of the pandemic. However, it is important to note that the money was primarily used to ensure that the two newly employed full-time administration staff were retained during the lockdown. It is a testament again to the standing of this little theatre that the government selected this playhouse as a venue it deemed necessary to save and protect with special funding during the pandemic.

The Equity Fringe Agreement is a recognition at least that things operate differently on the fringe. However, it does lay responsibility on the small production companies to make a profit, and this pushes companies towards monologues and two-handers, or receiving venues to look increasingly favourably on shows with considerable backing – which runs the risk of encouraging vanity projects from the affluent, possibly even dilettantes, which would not be healthy for the fringe. In all likelihood, for the fringe at least, the best way forward is to find funding from the private sector, or charitable trusts, which don't challenge the autonomy of the theatre and trust the fringe to allocate the money where it functions most fruitfully.

The literary department has been part of the Finborough's structure since the late 1980s, albeit rather informally at the outset. Noted former literary managers include playwrights Van Badham and Alexandra Wood. The fact that Finborough doesn't pay its readers or members of its literary team is lamentable, certainly. For the individuals that comprise the theatre's literary department, the organisation and hours involved in viewing shows and reading scripts takes up time obviously, and viewing shows is occasionally costly in terms of transport (though somewhat offset by free admission to shows). Most fringe theatres will not have a literary department in a formal sense, and those that do, generally receive Arts Council funding and so are equipped to run such a service. The Finborough doesn't receive this funding.

The Finborough's lack of payment does hold some advantages for those wishing to enter a career in theatre, nevertheless. The system has endured because for many emerging theatre industry workers, any experience gained at The Finborough can launch a paid career elsewhere. I know from first-hand experience. I would not have had the opportunity to be a literary manager or dramaturge at a prominent theatre in London had this been a paid role. In applying, I would have been competing with people with far more experience and qualifications than I had at that stage in my career. I was also a migrant, from Ireland, arriving in the UK via 12 years in Hungary and two in France. I knew no one in London and hadn't been at school or university with anyone of note in London theatre. In a country that operates greatly on social connections, this lack of contacts put me at a striking disadvantage. That I could find a position in a theatre and learn on the job was very valuable, and I was grateful for it.

When The Finborough looks for volunteers, the theatre doesn't absolutely require experience, rather it prioritises keenness to learn and an instinct for dramaturgy. Applicants must pass a set test in which plays are read and thoroughly assessed. This exercise ensures The Finborough can gauge if a potential reader has the knowledge and native dramaturgical understanding fundamental to the role, an ability to assess a play's potential, and that their tastes broadly chime with those of the theatre. The Finborough trains staff up in a hands-on way. This approach provides an access point for those without experience who wish to work in theatre but don't have the industry or social contacts, and/or the specific formal education and track record they would need to join a paid literary department elsewhere. Although some may argue that such volunteerism is a luxury only the more affluent can afford, this profile would not describe either myself or the majority of this theatre's literary department. I've described my own circumstances. The readers tend to be young, newly graduated writers, actors, directors, early career academics, or aspiring critics, also working a day job in a non-theatre industry to pay their rent. The volunteer system means The Finborough's literary department is relatively large with approximately 25 readers at any given time. Their number ensures that by and large, a volunteer's work for The Finborough's literary department takes up only a few hours per week and can be arranged around their own schedules.

As it is an unpaid position, and members are often seeking paid work in theatre elsewhere, the literary team has a high turnover of volunteers, and this is understood and accepted by all. The Finborough always supplies a good reference to help them on their way, so long as the reader actually carried out their allocated role. In this way, volunteers cut their teeth as script readers or literary team members at The Finborough, and then move on with their careers perhaps finding work as a reader with a funded theatre, their prospects improved by their time spent as a Finborough volunteer. If The Finborough were to obtain funds and provide a standard payment for all members of staff, this may change the situation and The Finborough may be required to find staff members with specific qualifications, allocate set hours, and put a cap on the numbers. It would change the situation and make the Finborough less of an accessible entry point. I fully appreciate that not everyone would agree with how this operates. Rebecca Mairs, literary manager at the Lyric Belfast for example, would counsel against readers agreeing to work as volunteers, particularly as she sees it as lessening the case for public funding for other literary departments: "I wouldn't suggest that aspiring playwrights get work as readers where possible. Don't offer to work for free as that diminishes the importance of the job. I'm really keen to see literary departments attain the funding needed."[12] I appreciate Mairs has a case, but the fact remains that if the Finborough had to pay readers today, the literary department would likely have to close and this I am convinced would be a loss to the theatre in London. I hope to see a time when the Finborough can afford to compensate readers at least some small amount. I would hope this funding would not come with restrictions attached, and that the theatre would continue to be a destination for outliers and outsiders as they attempt to enter the world of theatre in London.

The Finborough maintains a literary department as the theatre is dedicated to the goal of identifying, fostering, and nurturing talent which will go on to play a central role in the future of British theatre, be they writers, directors, designers, or actors. If The Finborough did not exist, British theatre would be the poorer today. Nonetheless, criticism of the theatre's failure to properly reward its creatives and members of its literary and production teams is understandable.

The Finborough might have some way to go in ensuring that it strikes the right balance in generating income, maintaining standards, and paying both its artists, literary department and theatre workers an acceptable wage – but its artistic director presents a keenness to achieve this eventuality. There is a sense that The Finborough has listened and that the theatre is travelling in the right direction. Whether this occurs remains to be seen; more pertinently it will be interesting to monitor if funding will have an adverse effect on programming, as McPherson fears it might, or a negative impact on the provision of experience, training, and development opportunities the theatre currently delivers so successfully for theatre makers, playwrights and literary department members alike.[13]

NOTES

1. "The Finborough Theatre has developed a reputation out of all proportion to its tiny size. It has played its part in the careers of many remarkable playwrights, directors, and actors" (*Financial Times*).
"The Finborough, the National Theatre of the fringe" (Sierz, A.).
"The Finborough has continued to plough a fertile path of new plays and rare revivals that gives it an influence disproportionate to its tiny 50-seat size" (Shenton, M. *The Stage*).
"No independent outfit turned out more regularly interesting surprises than The Finborough" (Dominic Dromgoole, *The Full Room*).
"The Finborough has … played a vital part…in the explosion of creativity in British theater in the 1990s. It was here that Max Stafford-Clark first glimpsed the potential of Mark Ravenhill" (Sierz, A. *In-Yer-Face Theatre*).
"Over the last three years, The Finborough has seriously rivalled the Royal Court, Hampstead and the Bush as a venue for new writing" (Michael Billlington, *The Guardian*).
2. Matt Wolf, *TheArtsDesk.com*, 9th July, 2020. https://theartsdesk.com/node/85489/view
3. National Portfolio Organisations (NPOs) refer to arts institutions funded by Arts Council England, with their expenditure is monitored over a four-year period. They include the Royal National Theatre and The Royal Court Theatre as well as museums, orchestras and galleries, for example.
4. Lyn Gardner, *The Guardian*, 21st May, 2010. https://www.theguardian.com/stage/theatreblog/2010/may/21/theatre-what-to-see
5. "The mighty little Finborough which… continues to offer a mixture of neglected classics and new writing in a cannily curated mix" (Gardner, L. *The Stage*, 2017).
6. The right to fail is a much vaunted policy of the English Stage Company at the Royal Court Theatre in London's Sloane Square. It emerged in the late 1950s when that theater was programming, the then, provocative and progressive kitchen sink plays such as John Osborne's *Look Back in Anger* (1956). The term is attributed to the director and one of the founding members of the English Stage Company at the Royal Court, Tony Richardson. He proposed this approach as a bold reaction to productions that had failed with the critics or at the box office. The Royal Court Theatre is a National Portfolio Organisation, in receipt of Arts Council England funding.
7. The 2020–2021 Equity recommended standard rate for stage performers is £495 per week or more, excluding commuting expenses and per diems.
8. https://www.equity.org.uk/getting-involved/campaigns/professionally-made-professionally-paid

9   The Equity Fringe Agreement launched in 2015, endeavours to ensure actors and theater-makers are paid at least the national minimum wage. The Arts Council National lottery Project Grants Payment Conditions, published in Oct. 2020, outlines that payments are conditional on their receipt and approval of any additional information (or payment conditions) requested. Such conditions commonly refer to reducing risks, confirmation of proposed artists involvement, confirmation of dates, confirmation of other funding and a statement of income and expenditure to be provided by an accountant. It endeavours to ensure actors and theatre-makers are paid at least the national minimum wage, if not the full Equity rate that would be expected for major production companies in the West End, for example. This agreement is one to which The Finborough encourages production companies to adhere.

10 I carry out my role of literary manager at the Finborough in a voluntary capacity, and do so in addition to my own work as a playwright, academic and lecturer in creative writing at the University of Lincoln. I began to work at this theatre initially as a reader and dramaturge and later as literary manager, and have remained for the past seven years. I have never received any compensation for my work at the theatre. The readers and members of the literary team are also unpaid. I took this position wanting to learn about the inner workings of London theatre, gain experience, expand my network and my knowledge and my connection to new writing. I am in favour of the Finborough finding a means to pay myself and the literary team, and am exploring ways to make this possible. Still, I appreciate that working at the Finborough, even in a voluntary capacity, has afforded me opportunities that would not have otherwise materialised.

11 The following clauses are now standard in all contracts between The Finborough and production companies:

> **84**. It is agreed that if The Company has enough money to pay the actors and stage manager Equity Fringe Agreement rates, that they will use and contract actors and stage managers on the Equity Fringe Agreement.
>
> **85**. In the event that the Company is paying less than Equity Fringe Agreement minimum to their actors and stage managers, the Company undertakes to:

A. Pay an equal profit share, splitting 100% of all and any profits, to everyone working on the production.
B. Operate an "Open Book" system of accounting for the production.
C. To follow as many of the clauses of the Equity Fringe Agreement as is practicable

(The Finborough Theatre's template contract as of October, 2020).

12 Sue Healy's interview with Rebecca Mairs, via Zoom, August 10, 2021.

13 Note that the research for this case study draws on my article Forty Years On: The Funding Conundrum at The Finborough, published in Comparative Drama's special edition on *London Theatre, Volume 56, Number 1&2, Spring Summer 2022*, pp. 179–198, edited by Mark O'Thomas, Harry Derbyshire and Nicholas Holden and published by Western Michigan University Press.

CHAPTER 8

Life after literary management

NEXT STEPS

The careers that beckon for the literary manager when they feel they've served their time in a literary department are as varied as those that lead them to this fascinating and rewarding job in the first instance.

Following nine years as literary manager at the Royal Court Theatre, Chris Campbell left Sloane Square. He first moved into publishing and became the editorial director at Oberon Books, until that publishing house was acquired by Bloomsbury a year later. Campbell has since returned to translation and acting. He outlines what he feels he gained from his time at the Court:

> [As literary manager] you get a full understanding of how theatre works. It broadens your understanding of the industry in every way. You could quite easily go on into freelance producing or teaching or dramaturgy or become an artistic director of a theatre, even if you are not a director, it is not unheard of to go that route. Many literary managers have come from the acting or writing industries and could return to those sectors, (though I'm not convinced writers make good literary managers as I fear their tastes are sometimes too narrow, too subjective).

Fleur Hebditch has little intention of moving on any time soon; she loves her work. Fleur Hebditch she sees her future options as:

> You could move into artistic directorship, or working with new writers in some capacity. Some may consider directing. You will often get to do a measure of directing when you have readings and scratch nights anyway. I feel very lucky that I have found this job, which I didn't know existed when I was starting out.

I have acquired so many skills, and so much know-how, understanding and awareness of all that is theatre from my time as literary manager at the Finborough. I hope this guide goes some way to sharing a least some of the knowledge I have gained from this position. Most importantly, however, is what the playwrights gain from having a literary manager at a theatre. It's for a playwright to provide the last word on the value of a literary manager. According to Simon Stephens[1]:

> Literary managers have empowered me to follow my instincts. They push and empower you to get to the story you want to tell.

Figure 8.1 Chris Campbell, Former Literary Manager, Royal Court Theatre, Now Returned to Acting. We Wish Him All the Best! Credit: Chris Campbell Archive.

NOTE

1 Sue Healy's interview with Simon Stephens, Brick Lane, London, August 13, 2021.

PART 2

THE LITERARY MANAGER AS TEACHER

A literary manager is tasked with developing talent. This duty is usually connected with the fostering of emerging playwrights keen to escalate their career to the next level. Sometimes, however, the literary manager might be invited to introduce the art of playwriting to the uninitiated; perhaps schoolchildren, or a youth group, or pensioners, or library group, or offenders in a local prison, or a centre for migrants, for example. Such scenarios will often involve educating these new writers in the craft of theatre from scratch, perhaps leading them in producing a devised piece of theatre. In this situation, the literary manager will be introducing novice playwrights to the world of creative writing for the first time and instructing them in the very basics of dramaturgy. Here, I refer to these as '**beginner**' classes.

On another level, the literary manager might wish to run workshops for more experienced playwrights, perhaps these are individuals who are keen theatre-goers and have attempted some short plays already but need direction and feedback as they hone their art and they might come to the theatre via an initiative the literary manager has launched. I call these learners '**intermediate.**'

More experienced playwrights might ask the literary manager to help them identify what is exciting or confusing in their play or unpick and test its structure for faults, examining scenes, timelines, character arcs, and dialogue styles. Or you may have a group of talented emerging writers specifically identified for development by the literary manager. These writers are '**advanced.**'

In each and all of these situations, the literary manager must take on the role of an educator. It is very useful to have a handy box of workshop topics and structured lesson plans on hand for each and every scenario. All materials can be adapted to all levels, however.

I have spent 20 years teaching creative writing and nowadays, I specialise in teaching dramatic writing. I've taught across Europe – largely in Hungary. In the

UK, my teaching experience spans prisons, in adult education colleges, theatres and, presently, at university level. I've also attended a great number of workshops with respected experts on narrative, story development, and dramaturgy. I've created, collected and adapted, and collated workshop materials throughout this time and added much from my own experience as an educator. The following materials and workshop suggestions are meant to be practical, accessible, easy-to-follow, and well-suited for the resourceful workshop facilitator who will add and adapt according to the needs and backgrounds of the participants. These are workshops I've found to be the most popular and beneficial and provide the most fruitful dramaturgical lessons. I have divided them into categories, though they can easily be adapted up or down depending on the levels and needs of the playwrights in the room. The main lesson for a beginner can be a swift warm-up for an advanced workshop, for example.

I was fortunate to have studied playwriting with the late dramaturge and playwright Stephen Jeffreys. His book *Playwriting: Structure, Character, How and What to Write* remains an invaluable lodestar of ideas for workshops and which I owe a great deal in my own teaching practice. I have also leaned into David Edgar's excellent *How Plays Work* when exploring the universality of stories. Other influences have come from workshops I've attended led by the renowned literary manager (ex-Royal Court Theatre) Graham Whybrow, and that noted supporter of playwrights, Greg Mosse (Criterion Theatre New Writing programme). Additionally, I owe a debt to the late screenwriter Gill Dennis, the American screen dramaturge whose London workshops I attended early in my career. All the above have helped shape my approach, my teaching materials, and informed my practice. I am grateful for having learned from their experience and creativity, and hope I give due credit where merited.

WORKSHOP 1

GETTING STARTED - inspiration - ABC Freewriting Exercise
Level: beginner **Time:** 90 mins to 2 hours **Notes:** Can work well with large groups
Goal: Introduce freewriting to new writers with little or no experience with writing creatively and to use their subconscious as a source of inspiration. Encourage them to write at some length without inhibition and gain confidence in their ability to come up with story ideas and identify aspects of an idea worth developing.
Objectives: Playwrights will understand how to source ideas from their own imaginations. Playwrights will demonstrate an understanding of the beginning, middle, and end. Playwrights will discuss what is good and what needs revising. Playwrights will learn how to recognise the potential in their freewriting. Playwrights will show an understanding of the importance of playfulness and risk-taking.
Materials: The alphabet is written out as a visual aid (on a board or projected). A handout (or written in a prominent position in the room) with the sentence: "The quick brown fox jumps over the lazy dog."
Introduction: Ask playwrights where they think their ideas might come from. Discuss ways to mine one's sub-conscious for ideas. Introduce the concept of freewriting. Discuss morning pages (credit Julia Cameron's *The Artists' Way*).
Warm-up Activity: Ask playwrights to write with pen and paper. Instruct them to use their non-dominant hand to write the following sentence: "The quick brown fox jumps over the lazy dog." Discuss why this sentence is special (all letters of the alphabet) and how this switch of hand makes them feel. Discuss the right side v. left side of the brain and how important it is to get the literal and the lateral in conversation.

Main Activity: Ask the playwrights to free-write a story using the alphabet as a frame. Explain that they will use the next letter of the alphabet as the first letter of each consecutive sentence. Give an example:

"**A**dam was hungry.

Because he'd run out of food, Adam decided to go to the shop.

Coincidentally, he bumped into his friend at the bus-stop.

David looked upset.

Even though Adam didn't like David much, he asked if he could help" (etc.)

Give a time limit of 30 minutes. Instruct playwrights not to worry about spelling, grammar, vocabulary, or even making much sense, but just to have fun and let the ideas flow. When time's up, instruct them to put down pens no matter where they are in the alphabet. Ask them to note three things they like in this story (explain that these can be characters, language, tone, humour, story idea, plot, dialogue, setting, and pace – anything at all). Ask them to share what they like about their story with the rest of the workshop. Elicit their thoughts on how they felt when writing and discuss "getting into the writing zone." Discuss how fruitful doing this sort of free-write every day.

Put into pairs. Instruct playwrights to share their stories with their partners. Instruct the partner to identify the beginning, the middle, and the end of the story. Ask the playwright if they agree.

Ask them to tidy up their story based on their own thoughts and feedback received.

Elicit their thoughts on their second draft. Ask if any would be comfortable sharing with the class.

Follow on: Ask playwrights to do this exercise every day for a week to build up a portfolio of ideas. Rather than use the alphabet as a frame each time, suggest they take a random sentence from a book and use the first letter of each word as a frame for their own free-write.

Summing up: Elicit thoughts on the usefulness of this freewriting exercise. Check that aims and objectives were met.

WORKSHOP 2

GETTING STARTED II – inspiration – ideas from real life
Level: beginner to intermediate **Time:** 2 hours+ **Notes:** Can be adapted for large and small groups.
Goal: Introduce playwrights to the concept of adapting stories from external sources. Playwrights will clarify and hone their understanding of a beginning, middle, and end. Introduce playwrights to a classic story structure.
Objectives: Playwrights will understand how to source ideas from their environment. Playwrights will demonstrate an understanding of the beginning, middle, and end. Playwrights will discuss how to identify good story potential. Playwrights will learn how to identify their protagonist's key desires. Playwrights will learn the basics of story adaptation.
Materials: Newspapers, magazines, access to internet, and websites such as Reddit. Try to have a diverse selection. Local papers and true crime magazines are a good starting point. Possibly provide the flash fiction of "For Sale, Baby Shoes, Never Worn," attributed to Hemmingway, as a means of demonstrating how even a small ad can suggest a story.
Introduction: Discuss external sources for stories – make a list (on a board/flip chart/smart board). A sample list might include: Family history Gossip Jokes The news (newspapers, magazines, websites, social media) Discuss the importance of "not being a snob about stories" – and that often the best story ideas can come from tabloids or true crime magazines.
Warm-up Activity: Ask playwrights to look through newspapers for an interesting story. Encourage them to look for shorter, simple, and unusual stories. Ask them to share this story with the class. Encourage them to feedback on the drama value of each story.

Main Activity: If the number of playwrights in the workshop is large, split them into smaller groups of three or four playwrights each. Ask each group to select one story for the group to work on. If the number of playwrights in the class is small, have them work individually.

Explain the importance of the protagonist having a desire that drives the story. Introduce the 'three Ds' of Desire + Danger = Drama. Explain a desire can be great (they want to rule the world) or small (they want to get to the shop for milk before it closes). Have the playwrights identify their protagonist's desires?

Introduce a classic story structure, explaining each step (use the helpful graphs for teaching story structure on pages 161–164).

Instruct the group to fit their story into this frame. Give a time limit of 30 mins.

Have the playwrights pitch their story idea to their peers. Provide feedback.

Discuss the legal implications of using real-life stories and elicit ideas of how to change aspects of the story so it is no longer identifiable. Suggest perhaps changing the nationality of gender or setting or time of year – and consider what these changes would take or give to the story.

With feedback and ideas for adaptation in hand, instruct the playwrights to write a short pitch for their story.

Follow on: Ask playwrights to do this exercise at home with a single story every day for a week. Suggest they choose their favourite on the weekend and develop the short pitch into a more detailed overview.

Summing up: Elicit thoughts on the usefulness of this exercise. Check that aims and objectives were met.

WORKSHOP 3

GIVING MEANING – theme – proverbs and symbols
Level: beginner – intermediate*
Time: 60–90 mins
Notes: Works best with young learners, and diverse groups from various cultural backgrounds. *Can be adapted to advanced level with a discussion on Saussure and semiotics and an exploration of themes in contemporary works.
Goal: Introduce the use or theme or message in a story and consider ways to incorporate them in a play. Playwrights consider how they view reality and identify how they might communicate these beliefs via metaphor. This topic might work best with younger playwrights, although it can be adapted for all ages.
Objectives: Playwrights will demonstrate an understanding of the use of metaphor in storytelling.   Playwrights will demonstrate an understanding how to deploy symbols in their work.   Playwrights will identify theme in classic plays (or stories, or films).   Playwrights will identify their own worldview.
Materials: A list of proverbs that can be added to by the students (board or projected).   A handout or projected images of a vanitas painting, full of symbols.   A handout of an Aesop's fable, or two.
Introduction: Tell playwrights you're going to explore theme. Elicit their knowledge of theme. Ask if they can identify the themes in *Romeo and Juliet* (the power of romantic love, the power of hatred), or *Othello* (racism, manipulation, jealousy), or perhaps well-known films if they're not that familiar with theatre.

Warm-up Activity: Read out or give them handouts to read of an Aesop's fable or an old parable. An example:

The Scorpion and The Frog

> A scorpion wishes to cross a river but can't swim. It asks a frog for a piggy back to the other side. The frog refuses saying the scorpion might sting it. The scorpion argues that he'd be stupid to do so, as they'd both drown. The frog sees the sense in this point, relents and accepts the scorpion as a passenger. Midway across the river, the scorpion stings the frog, dooming them both. The dying frog asks the scorpion why he did it, as they would both now die. The scorpion replies that it couldn't help it, to sting and kill is a scorpion's nature.

(other possible stories – The Tortoise and the Hare, Appointment in Samarra)

Ask students if they can identify what the story is about and what is the theme? What does this story tell the world? Ask if they agree with the message.

Main Activity: Discuss the theme. Consider the difference between reportage and story-telling as art. Discuss how artists communicate their understanding of reality, their worldview, their philosophy. Give other examples of metaphor and allegory (e.g. *Animal Farm*).

Introduce the idea of the proverb, a simple traditional saying that is philosophy in a nutshell. Give some examples of very well-known proverbs and ask them to explain their meaning. Instruct students to note down a proverb. It doesn't necessarily have to be one they agree with, it might make them smile, or they might very much disagree with it. In a culturally diverse group, this can be a very informative exercise. Many proverbs have a similar version, but not the same, in other languages and cultures. Write up the proverbs provided by the students, adding to a list you've prepared already. A sample selection of proverbs:

Graveyards are full of indispensable people

You can catch more flies with honey than you can with vinegar

A little learning is a dangerous thing

The belly has no ears

Trees don't grow to the sky

A dumb priest never got a parish

The only free cheese is in the mousetrap

Eaten bread is soon forgotten

The squeaky door gets the oil

Tell playwrights to select a proverb that appeals. Instruct them to note the theme and write out the message in simple language. For example, the first proverb listed here is a comment on the danger of hubris or pride. Ask the students to use a story frame to sketch out a story idea to demonstrate this theme in action (do explain that they are free to use a counter stance, e.g. hubris is good, if they wish). Tell them to identify the protagonist and their desire. Give a time limit of 30 mins.

Introduce the concept of symbols. Show a vanitas painting filled with symbols representing (say) the passing of time, deception, and industry. Draw a list of themes and their classical counterparts. For example:

Moon – Femininity

Lemon – Deception

Dog – Loyalty

Moth – Addiction

Candle – Enlightenment

Bee – Industry

Green – Jealousy

Forget-Me-Not – Remembrance

Daffodil – Narcissism

Silver coins – Betrayal

Instruct students to decide on a symbol for their theme and incorporate that symbol into their story idea.

Put into pairs. Instruct playwrights to share their story idea with their partner. Ask the partner to explain the story idea (in this way the playwright gets a sense of what sticks and what doesn't in their pitch).

Ask them to tidy up their story idea based on their own thoughts and feedback received.

Elicit their thoughts on their second draft. Ask if any would be comfortable sharing with the class.

Follow on: Ask playwrights to revisit older work for theme.

Summing up: Elicit thoughts on the usefulness of this exercise. Check that aims and objectives were met.

WORKSHOP 4

SHAPING STORY – adaptation – bare-bones stories
Level: intermediate
Time: 90 mins to 2 hours
Notes: Can work well with large groups
Goal: Reinforce the classic story structure, using classical bare-bones fairytales as a frame. Instruct learners on how they might adapt these fantastical tales into more realistic contemporary stories.
Objectives: Playwrights will understand that there is no such thing as a new story. Playwrights will demonstrate an understanding of the beginning, middle, and end. Playwrights will identify what story elements can be adapted and what cannot. Playwrights will demonstrate an understanding of catharsis. Playwrights will prepare a short professional pitch.
Materials: A selection of fairy tales or well-known stories as handouts – written bare-bones are a few lines only. For example: They want rid of the rats and he gets rid of them. They refuse to pay him. He takes their children. *(Pied Piper of Hamlin)* She wants to go to the ball, but is forbidden. She goes eventually, but has to leave early. She goes finally and gets the Prince. *(Cinderella)* He's black and she's white and they love each other passionately but he has an enemy. He becomes jealous – she becomes worried. He kills her. *(Othello)*

Introduction: Revise what might be known of story structure. Write prominently Stephen Jeffreys' reference of "the beginning, the muddle and the end." Have visible the legend: "conflict, crisis and resolution." Handout a useful story frame if needed. Discuss the importance of danger, of muddle, of conflict, in drama. Conflict arises when someone wants something and someone else or something tries to stop them from getting it – discuss. The desire must be intense and the danger a great obstacle.

Warm-up Activity: Hand out the bare-bones stories. A selection might include: *Little Red Riding Hood, Goldilocks and the Three Bears, Snow White and the Seven Dwarves, Hansel and Gretel, Rapunzel, The Three Little Pigs, Beauty and the Beast, Sleeping Beauty.*

Main Activity: Ask the playwrights to identify the story in their handout. Instruct them to ring-fence the beginning, the middle, and the end. Ask them to identify the protagonist's desire. Guide them on noting the extent to which the protagonist has changed by then end of the story (catharsis).

Using a story frame, ask the playwrights to plot the story on that structure. Give a time limit of 20–30 mins.

Instruct playwrights to adapt the story so that it is realistic by adapting the story to a believable modern setting, with realistic modern problems. The three little pigs, for example, might be three brothers attempting to get on the housing ladder. Sleeping Beauty might be in a coma. Rapunzel might be trafficked as a sex worker. Hansel and Gretel might have a close shave with a paedophile. Encourage them to update the names (Rowan and Julia) (Enzo and Grace) (Sindy Ellison) and place them in a familiar locale (Red Hudd lives in the New Forest). Explain they can change everything except the theme or the heart of the story.

Give a time limit of 20–30 mins.

Instruct playwrights to write a pitch for their work using this frame:

This is a story about (describe your main character) who (provide their desire) **BUT** (identify the overwhelming obstacle that prevents the realisation of their goal). And then, in one line, state why this story is personally important to you.

Ask the playwrights to present their adaptation to the class, clearly pin-pointing the 'beginning, muddle, end.' See if their peers recognise the original story. Ask peers to give feedback – and instruct that it's presented in a sandwich form ('positive, negative, positive' – or 'cuddle, punch, cuddle').

Ask playwrights to tidy up their stories based on their own thoughts and feedback received.

Elicit their thoughts on their second draft. Ask if any would be comfortable sharing with the class.

Follow on: Ask playwrights to do this exercise every day for a week to build up a portfolio of modernised fairy tales.
Summing up: Elicit thoughts on the usefulness of this exercise. Check that aims and objectives were met.

WORKSHOP 5

DEVELOPING CHARACTERS - a question of character
Level: intermediate – advanced
Time: 2 hours+
Notes: Can work well with large groups
Goal: Encourage writers to develop rounded, interesting, empathetic, and believable characters with a single desire.
Objectives: Playwrights will create complicated and layered characters. Playwrights will identify clichéd characters. Playwrights will show an understanding of the need for a character to desire something. Playwrights will use an array of tools to develop characters.
Materials: A list of the seven deadly sins. The character traits of the 12 astrological signs. Examples of clichéd character types (dumb blonde, boring accountant, organised German) Images of Van Gogh's chair portraits. A list of character questions – dating sites are good sources for these kinds of questions.
Introduction: Get students to name some memorable characters from the canon, classic thru contemporary: Lady Macbeth, Romeo, Willy Loman, Johnny 'Rooster' Byron, and Fleabag. If students are not very familiar with theatre, elicit their knowledge of characters from books or films (Harry Potter, James Bond, Doctor Who, etc.). Ask students to briefly describe some of these characters.
Warm-up Activity: Show on projection or handout: Van Gogh's chair portraits of himself and of Paul Gauguin. Ask the writers to identify what Van Gogh is saying about himself in his self-portrait chair, and what he's saying about Gauguin in that chair portrait (possibly that Van Gogh is down-to-earth, a simple peasant at heart, whilst Gauguin is sophisticated, learned, and slightly dark). Ask them to consider if this is a true description of either. Introduce the concept of a Mary Sue (a flawless character) and discuss the issues with such an invention.

Main Activity: Make a list of flaws. Stephen Jeffreys suggests the seven deadly sins for this topic (sloth, wrath, lust, envy, gluttony, avarice, and pride, with the addition of hypocrisy). Equally, the playwrights could describe what they like least in people (meanness, sharp-tongued, domineering, inconsiderate, etc.) and ask them to consider adding this flaw to a good character. Ask your learners to think of yin and yang – any overly good character should have little flaw to make them interesting, and any nasty character should have a redemptive element that allows for some empathy. Warn your writers that any character based on themselves is always in danger of falling into a Mary Sue trap. Describe some clichéd characters and discuss why these characters are problematic. Encourage students to come up with ways to upend clichés.

Hand out a list of questions for your character. You could do one with the class having (say) Lady Macbeth answering the questions. A sample list of questions could include:

What is their superstition?

What does their best friend think of them?

What are they like when they get drunk?

What do they keep in their bedside drawer?

What is their favourite joke?

What is their biggest fear?

Also, ask them to make notes as to their character's:

Nickname

Gender

Age

Looks

Education level

Socio-economic background

Marital status

Diet

Ethnicity

Unique physical trait

Ask the playwrights to decide on their character's star-sign, then handout the descriptions for each zodiac sign. Instruct the learners to go over all their notes and draw up a clear description of their character. Allow 20–30 minutes for this exercise. (Note Stephen Jeffreys suggests the Meyers–Briggs test).

Put into pairs or groups of three or four. Instruct playwrights to describe/introduce their character to others. Then, tell the group that all their characters are stuck in a lift together (it doesn't matter if one is a medieval knight and another a Victorian ghost, just go with it). Decide what happens. Who has a panic attack? Who is the hero? Who has a fight? Who falls in love?

Elicit what they have learned about their character from this exercise. Explain how placing your character in a tense situation can reveal much.

Follow on: Ask the playwrights to have their character email another character in the lift, asking for a favour. Instruct them to allow their characters voice to come through.

Summing up: Elicit thoughts on the usefulness of this exercise. Check that aims and objectives were met.

WORKSHOP 6

ACTIVE DIALOGUE – subtext, dynamism, and agency

Level: intermediate to advanced

Time: 60–90 mins

Notes: Useful for revision of dialogue and development of subtext on works-in-progress. I was introduced to using transitive verbs in this way by literary manager Graham Whybrow, on an Arvon Course in April 2014. I have since developed and adapted the concept to fit my own teaching materials, but the essential concept of using transitive verbs to help playwrights understand how to use subtext to drive a scene is credited to Whybrow.

Goal: Reinforce students' awareness of the need for characters to have agency and facilitate their checking for the same in their editing and revising process. To identify the dangers of passive characters. To shore-up students' understanding of subtext in dialogue. Identify issues surrounding exposition.

Objectives:

Playwrights will develop their ability to show rather than tell in dialogue, using subtext.

Playwrights will demonstrate an appreciation of active characters with agency.

Playwrights will edit and address exposition heavy dialogue.

Playwrights will show an understanding of the transitive verbs under-riding each scene.

Materials:

A handout of transitive verbs (or displayed on a smart board) – sample sheet provided below.

Introduction: Introduce the idea of an active character with a desire and a plan and intention, and a passive character who gets aimlessly blown about the story like a leaf in the wind. Explain that in good drama, characters are always doing something to each other, the protagonist must have agency, and that each scene should be driven by an under-riding desire. Discuss the director Max Stafford-Clark's use of 'actioning.'

Warm-up Activity: Explain what transitive verbs are: A transitive verb is a verb that takes an object (X verbs Y (X is the subject, Y is the object)). Dramaturgically, we understand this as Character X 'does something to' Character Y. Give examples of transitive verbs: Winston tricks Joseph. Anne embarrasses Fatima. Delores snubs Declan. For clarity, provide examples of intransitive verbs: Saoirse walks. Liz shops. Alfreddo hunts. Ask playwrights to write three sentences of their own using *transitive* verbs.

Main Activity: Distribute the handout of transitive verbs. Choose short scenes from a selection of contemporary plays. Ask playwrights to work in pairs to establish what the dominant transitive verb is in this scene. Playwrights then present to class. Discussion.

Lead discussion in describing how the action is communicated via subtext, rather than exposition. Ask playwrights to re-write the short scene by removing the subtext and replacing it with exposition. Rather than veiled threats and back-handed insults, you should result in something like: "Hello, I'm Molly, I'm here to make you feel small and insignificant," "Hi Molly, please don't do that. Feel sorry for me, my girlfriend has dumped me." "She had sense. You're stupid." "But I've got lots of money, which you love." "I do! OK, I'll try to like you for the sake of the money." "Go away. You're superficial." Clearly, this has comic potential – but ensure playwrights consider how this doesn't work in terms of serious dramatic dialogue.

Instruct playwrights to consider a scene in their own works-in-progress and identify the transient verb that is under-riding the scene. Ask them to consider the subtext. Discourage them from using 'wrylies' (adverbs in parenthesis that tell the actors how to deliver the lines – such as: sarcastically, archly, and wryly). Insist instead that the subtext should be clear to the director and actors from the dialogue. Encourage the playwrights to trust the professionalism of the director and actors.

Reinforce and revise understanding of how this exercise is useful when revising and testing sections, ensuring the text is dynamic and the protagonist is not passive.

Follow on: Encourage playwrights to go through their entire text noting the transitive verbs under-riding each scene.

Summing up: Elicit thoughts on the usefulness of this exercise. Check that aims and objectives were met.

WORKSHOP 7

SETTING – GENRE – playing with the cliche   **Level:** Intermediate – advanced   **Time:** 2 hours   **Notes:** Can be adjusted to advanced level by examining the role of the scene's duration, and scrutinising open space/closed space, and what this will mean for your characters. Consider the work of Beckett (*Waiting for Godot*, *Happy Days*).
Goal: Explore using setting as a character and the impact it can have on a story. Consider what setting lends atmosphere, plot, and theme. Encourage students to think outside the box, and not to set all their plays around a kitchen table.
Objectives: Playwrights will understand how the setting can provide plot twists, surprises, and challenges.   Playwrights will demonstrate an understanding of pathetic fallacy.   Playwrights will discuss using the senses playwriting.   Playwrights will consider what should be included in stage directions, and what is best left to the director and set designer.   Playwrights will show an understanding of the importance of playfulness and risk-taking.
Materials: Pictures of diverse settings.
Introduction: Discuss what a closed setting, with trapped characters, might lend a play. Similarly, lead a discussion on what an open space might provide (the ease of characters arriving unannounced, and leaving similarly).   Show pictures. Instruct students to sort into closed/open spaces.   Discuss clichéd settings (castle on a dark and stormy night) and genre expectations. Ask students to consider upending the cliché.
Warm-up Activity: Ask playwrights to make a list of genres (examples):   Historical   Children's   Gothic   Chekhovian realism   Noir   Horror

Kitchen Sink

Farce

In-yer-face

French window

Pantomime

Instruct playwrights to note down the setting most usually associated with this genre. For example:

Kitchen Sink – a working-class kitchen.

In-yer-face – a flat share

Chekhovian realism – a rural house with a family

Gothic – a castle

Do as many as makes sense with the group's size. Consider clichés and ask the group what can be gained by challenging a cliché?

Ask students to name the five senses. Discuss how the setting can be experienced by all senses. Suggest they incorporate smell and touch, actors will use gesture to communicate these.

Main Activity: Divide into groups (or pairs) and provide each with a genre. Have learners select a setting randomly, from the lucky dip. This approach will result in strange bedfellows (historical play set in a swimming pool?) but ask them to go with it – to discuss how it might work and the advantages of this setting. Tell them to consider entrances and exits and measure how 'free' the cast are.

Provide a story frame/structure (see pages 161–164) and ask the group to use as a scaffold for mapping out a story. Ask them to properly use the setting and embrace the challenges and limitations and opportunities it might bring. Tell them to consider using a time of day they wouldn't normally opt for (midnight, dawn, lunchtime, etc.). Make sure that they are not afraid to play with the setting. The swimming pool can be empty, for example. Ask them to think about the metaphor.

When done, each group presents to the class. They discuss what they found surprising, or limiting, and what they have taken from the exercise.

Follow on: Ask playwrights to revisit their work-in-progress, and consider the setting – can it be changed? Can it be moved to another time of day? Can setting play a greater part?

Summing up: Elicit thoughts on the usefulness of this exercise. Check that aims and objectives were met.

WORKSHOP 8

DIALOGUE – was it something I said? – editing dialogue
Level: intermediate- advanced
Time: 90 mins
Notes: This workshop is a good follow-up to the workshop on transitive verbs, or can be merged with it for advance levels.
Goal: Impart to the playwrights how to identify when dialogue is necessary, and when it's not. Reinforce their understanding of the pitfalls of exposition, of including unnecessary dialogue. Encourage them to write dialogue with confidence, and to use subtext. Encourage playwrights to trust the actor and director.
Objectives: Playwrights will understand plays are written to be performed, not read by the public. Playwrights will demonstrate an understanding of subtext. Playwrights will discuss what to keep and what to delete in terms of dialogue. Playwrights will show they recognise exposition. Playwrights will identify times when silence is the best thing to say.
Materials: If possible, a recording of people chatting is useful – the more inane the banter, the better. And better still, if full of hesitation and fillers and non-sequiturs, unfinished sentences, and waffles. A sample of dialogue from a senior contemporary playwright (Simon Stephens, debbie tucker greene, Caryl Churchill would be a good choice. Don't select a monologue. Stick to a dialogue where speech is crisp, spare, and reliant on subtext). Copies of the opening scene of Lucy Kirkwood's *The Children*.
Introduction: Ask playwrights why they never see anyone politely say good bye on a telephone call in the movies (because it's a waste of words – it doesn't move the story forwards). Explain that all dramatic dialogue should have a purpose, it should not be waffle, filling space on the page, delivering exposition and back-story. We rely on subtext, gesture, and suggestion for this.

Draw a fish on the board/flip chart if possible (simple line drawing!). Erase its head and tail – and explain that the meat of your scene is always in the middle. Advise playwrights to think of a scene this way – enter late and leave early. Draw their attention to the opening scene for Lucy Kirkwood's *The Children* where, at curtain's rise 'Rose' stands in a kitchen, blood running from her nose speaking to an off-stage 'Hazel.' Their chat seems friendly enough, but something odd and violent has occurred. The audience is hooked and guessing. It wouldn't have been as impactful if the audience had witnessed Hazel strike Rose.

Warm-up Activity: Play the real-life dialogue. Ask playwrights what the discussion is about (a trick question really, as the banter is likely not to be about much). Ask them to write the dialogue down verbatim, in script form. Don't choose a long recording for this – just a few lines will make the point. Encourage them to perform the scene. Ask for feedback on the text. Tell them to put this script aside.

Main Activity: Introduce the contemporary text you've chosen. As a group, read through and identify the subtext (i.e. transitive verbs). Ask them what they think occurred just before and after this scene. Ask them why they think the playwright didn't include this information in the scene.

Put them in pairs. Ask them to compare the contemporary text with the verbatim dialogue script. How is it similar? How does it differ? Why is this?

Instruct the playwrights to edit down their verbatim text, cutting out waffle, fillers, repetition, non-sequiturs, and exposition. What is left? Ask them to add subtext and consider what actions might imply this subtext.

Instruct them to perform the text again.

How is it different from their first performance?

Reinforce the fact that less is more.

Follow on: Encourage playwrights to note down real conversations on a bus/train/café – and see what they would have to edit out to make it work dramatically. Explain that monologues have their place in theatre, but they're tricky and take skill and expertise to execute well. For the most part, good drama is about saying less, and the loudness of what you don't say.

Tips to pass on: Don't write accents phonetically, especially if not your own accent. You'll get it wrong, and you may offend. It's enough to indicate an accent in parenthesis (i.e., in a French accent).

Read your work aloud, feel its rhythms and potential trip-ups.

Don't use dialogue to refer to an action that happened in the past or off-stage. Keep action on stage and in the present.

Summing up: Elicit thoughts on the usefulness of this exercise. Check that aims and objectives were met.

WORKSHOP 9

UNIVERSAL STORIES – magic number 9
Level: advanced
Time: 90 mins to 2 hours
Notes: This workshop draws greatly on the work of Stephen Jeffreys' *Playwriting: Structure, Character, How and What to Write* and David Edgar's *How Plays Work*. You would be greatly advised to read these books before this workshop and encourage your students to do so afterwards. This workshop can neatly follow on from Workshop 4 and can be merged with it for a longer session.
Goal: Introduce the concept of a finite number of stories to the playwrights. Explain this knowledge is not to make their attempt to write original work seem futile, but rather to reassure them that there are structures, a scaffold, they can use and their play's originality will be the colour their own voice will bring to the story.
Objectives: Playwrights will understand they can learn from classic story structures, and use them. Playwrights will demonstrate an understanding of these structures. Playwrights will explore universal story structures and their similarities. Playwrights will accept there is no such thing as a 'new' story. Playwrights will demonstrate a willingness to be playful with form.
Materials: See pages 161–164 for additional teaching materials for David Edgar's 'Audiences' from his book *How Plays Work*. Also, Stephen Jeffreys' *'Nine Stories' chart*, from his book *Playwriting: Structure, Character, How and What to Write*.
Introduction: Discuss the idea that there are only two stories in the world – "Stranger comes to town" and "Hero sets out on a journey". Do students agree? Ask them if they can think of any films/plays/books that seem to tell the same story. See what their thoughts are on this point. Suggest that human-kind have been telling each other the same stories since we could speak. What are their thoughts on this? Discuss the stories that influenced Shakespeare's work. Does the fact that Shakespeare adapted these tales make him any less of a playwright?

Warm-up Activity: Distribute (or read aloud) the abridged extract from Edgar's book. Ask students to identify the stories. Give them the answers. Do they agree? Can they think of others that could be described by Edgar's descriptions?

Main Activity: Introduce/distribute Jeffreys' 'Nine Stories' frame. Put students into pairs and explain in further detail each type of story in Jeffreys' chart. Answer their questions.

Ask the students to think of their favourite play (or movie) and see where it might most comfortably fit on this chart. Consider their own work (if they've written any yet) and see if they can identify what type of story they lean towards.

Explain this exercise can help them see their work in a fresh light, and give them fodder for thought if they've hit a wall. If, for example, you realise your story is a Faustian one – then this exercise might make it clearer that you've got to deliver a bad ending.

Ask the students to consider a play (or movie) that they have identified as a specific type of story. Instruct them to note down in simple note form what happens in Act. I, Act II, and Act III. Direct them to play around with this approach, shuffle the acts around, go backwards through the story. What does this lend the piece?

Ask them to do the same with their own work in progress.

Invite them to share what they've discovered with the rest of the workshop.

Follow on: Encourage playwrights to read the following books:

Edgar, David (2009) **How Plays Work**, London, NHB.

Jeffreys, Stephen (2019) **Playwriting: Structure, Character, How and What to Write**, London: NHB

Vogler, Christopher (2007) **The Writers Journey: Mythic Structure for Writers**, New York: Michael Weise.

McKee, Robert (1999) **Story**: **Substance, Structure, Style and the Principles of Screenwriting** York, Methuen.

Waters, Steve (2010) **The Secret Life of Plays**, London: NHB.

Summing up: Elicit thoughts on the usefulness of this exercise. Check that aims and objectives were met.

Useful teaching materials

Stephen Jeffreys' nine stories

	Tend to End Well	**Neutral**	**Tend to End Badly**
Beginnings	Romeo & Juliet (*love across the barricades*)	Orpheus (*opens with something has been lost, often a person*)	Jacob & Esau (*sibling rivalry*)
Middle	Circe (*the pursuit story*)	Tristan and Iseult (*the love triangle*)	Achilles (*the fatal flaw*)
End	Cinderella (*good overcomes evil*)	Hercules (*the hero who never gives up*)	Faust (*the debt that must be paid*)

From David Edgar's *How Plays Work*

QUESTIONS

To which well-known tales do these descriptions refer?

1) Two sisters are unjustly preferred over a third younger sister. Despite their best efforts, the younger sister marries into royalty and the wicked sisters are confounded.

2) A town is threatened by a malevolent force of nature. A leading citizen takes the necessary action to protect this town, but finds that the economic interests are against him and he battles alone.

3) With her father's encouragement a young woman allows herself to be wooed by a prince. Her brother moves a long way away. The prince behaves badly toward his wife. She goes mad, alarms the royal family, gives everyone flowers, escapes from her minders and dies in a suspicious accident. The brother returns, angry, at the head of a popular army. There is a contest over the funeral arrangements between family, church and state. The prince and the brother fight over her coffin.

ANSWERS:

1) *King Lear and Cinderella.*
2) *Jaws and Ibsen's An Enemy of the People.*
3) *Hamlet and the death of Princess Diana.*

A STORY SCAFFOLD

a. The **world as it is**. The reader is introduced to the character and setting.
b. **Inciting incident** Something occurs which upsets the normal run of things. For example, a stranger arrives in town.
c. **The main character** is affected by this disturbance.
d. The main character decides on a **plan of action** to rectify or improve matters.
e. **Obstacles** stand in the way of the plan of action succeeding.
f. **Complications** occur in the guise of choices/new characters/new ideas/discovery
g. These lead to an unavoidable **crisis**.
h. The crisis usually leads to a **climax** or confrontation.
i. Finally comes the resolution, which results in a new state for the world.
j. The main character has learned a lesson.

BONUS ACTIVITY USING THE STORY SCAFFOLD

Using the story scaffold, instruct students to label the following graph. Either draw on a board/flip chart or distribute as hand-outs.

Ask students to divide the graph in three, into what they believe to be act I, act II and act III.

Identify a story (play/film/book) known to all students (The chosen story will often depend on the age and education level of the students. Some suggestions: *Romeo & Juliet/Titanic/Cinderella/Jerusalem*). Divide students into groups and ask them to unpack the narrative architecture of the story, identifying the particular aspects of its trajectory.

Instruct them to present their findings.

Discuss.

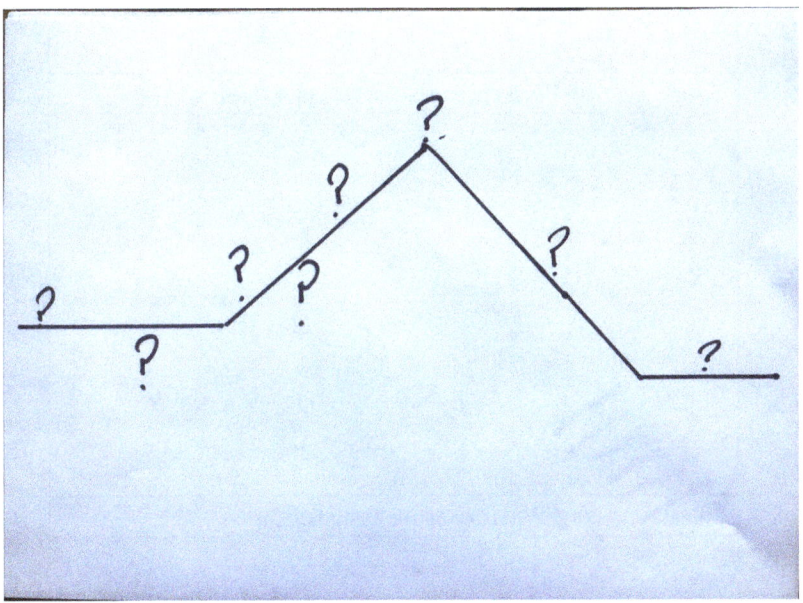

KNOW YOUR STORY

Exposition	What is the world of the story? Here is where you establish background information (setting, characterisation) that is important to the plot of the story. Make note of what is the worst thing that can happen to your protagonist, within the context of the story.
Inciting incident	What lights the blue touch paper? What occurs to set your story in motion?
Crisis	List the issues that lead up to the climax:
Climax	What is your play's high point?

Outcome	List the outcomes of the crisis.
Resolution	Does your main character achieve their goal?
Resolution	Does your play have a resolution? How are the endings tied up? Are they changed?

TRANSITIVE VERBS

Acuse, admire, admonish, adore, advise, aggravate, agitate, aid, alarm, alert, alienate, allure amaze amuse, anger, analyse, animate, annoy, antagonise, appal, appease, applaud, arouse, assist, assure, astonish, astound, attack, attract, awaken, avoid.

Baffle, bait, badger, banish, befriend, beg, beguile, belittle, berate, beseech, bewilder, bewitch, blame, bless, block, bolster, boost, boss, bribe, bully.

Cajole, calm, captivate, capture, caress, castigate, catch, caution, challenge, charm, chastise, cheer, cherish, chide, chill, coax, coerce, comfort, command, compel, compliment, condemn, confront, confuse, congratulate, conquer, control, contradict, convince, correct, corrupt, councel, counter, criticise, cross-examine, crucify, crush, cuddle, curse.

Damn, Dampen, dare Transitive, dazzle, debase, deceive, defend, deflate, deflect, defy, degrade, deify, delay, delight, demean, demolish, denigrate, denounce, deny, depress, deride, dispatch, destroy, divert, devastate, dignify, diminish, direct, disappoint, disarm, discard, discipline, disconcert, discourage, disdain, disgust, dishearten, dismiss, disparage, dissuade, distance, distress, disturb, divert, dodge, dominate, doubt, dumbfound, drag, dupe,

Educate, elevate, electrify, embarrass, embrace, empower, enchant, encourage, energise, enlighten, enlist, enliven, ennoble, enrage, ensnare, entertain, enthral, enthuse, entice, entrap, entreat, entrust, evade, exalt, examine, exasperate, excite, exclude, exhort, expel, expose. Fascinate, find, flatten, flatter, fluster, fondle, fool, force, forgive fortify, freak, frighten, frustrate, fire. Glorify, goad, grab, gratify, greet, grip, grope, guard, guide.

Halt, hammer, harangue, harm, harass, hassle, hasten, heckle, help, hide, hit, hold, hoodwink, horrify, hound, hug, humble, humiliate, humour, hurry hurt, hypnotise.

Ignore, imitate, ignore, impress, incite, Indoctrinate, infuriate, inspect, instruct, insult, interest, interrogate, intimidate, intrigue, invigorate, invite, involve, irritate.

Jeer, join, jolly, jolt, josh.

Kiss, kill, Lead, lecture, lighten, lure.

Manipulate, massage, menace, mesmerise, mock, molest, mollify, mollycoddle, mortify, mother, mystify.

Nag, nail, nauseate, needle, nurse, nuzzle,

Obey, oblige, obstruct, offend, offer, ogle, oppress, order, organise, ostracise, outsmart, outrage, outwit, overpower, override, overrule, overwhelm, oppose.

Pacify, pamper, panic, patronize, perplex, persecute, persuade, pester, petition, petrify, placate, please, poke, praise, prepare, press, pressurize, probe, procure, prod, prompt, protect, provoke, pulverise, punch, punish, pursue.

Quash, question, quieten, quiz

Rally, rape, rattle, ravage, ravage, reassure, rebuff, rebuke, refuse, recruit, reject, rejuvenate, renounce, repel, reprimand, reproach, repulse, rescue, resist, restore, restrain, revive, revolt, reward, ridicule, rile, rouse.

Sadden, savage, scandalize, scare, scorn, scold, scratch, seduce, seize, settle, shake, shame, shield, shock, sicken, silence, slander, slap, smash, smother, snub, soften, solicit, smooth, spurn, squash, stab, stalk, stall, startle, stop, simulate, sting, stir, strike, stroke, study, stun, stupefy, subdue, summon, support, suppress, survey, suspect, surprise,

Tame, tantalize, taunt, teach, tease, tempt, terrify, terrorise, test, threaten, thrill, tickle, titillate, torment, torture, touch, trap, trick, trouble

Undermine, undress, unsettle, upset, urge, usher.

Victimize and vilify.

Warm, warn, weaken, welcome, wheedle, woo, worry, worship

Bibliography

Bolton, J. *Demarcating Dramaturgy, Mapping Theory onto Practice* (2011). https://etheses.whiterose.ac.uk/3315/

Bourdieu, P. *Outline of a Theory of Practice* (Cambridge: Cambridge University Press, 1977).

Bourdieu, P. *Distinction: A Social Critique of the Judgement of Taste* (London: Routledge, 1984).

Bourdieu, P. *The Forms of Capital: Handbook of Theory and Research for the Sociology of Capital* (New York: Greenwood Press, 1986).

Bourdieu, P. *The Logic of Practice* (Redwood City: Stanford University Press, 1990).

Bourdieu, P. Goody, J (ed.), Nice, R. (Trans) (1977) *Outline of a Theory of Practice* (Cambridge Studies in Social and Cultural Anthropology) (Cambridge: Cambridge University Press, 1990).

Cattaneo, A. *The Art of Dramaturgy* (New Haven, CT: Yale University Press, 2021).

Edgar, D. *How Plays Work* (London: NHB, 2009).

Fisher, M. *How to Write About Theatre: A Manual for Critics, Student and Bloggers* (London: Bloomsbury Methuen, 2015).

Fuchs, E. *EF's Visit to a Small Planet: Some Questions to Ask a Play* (Durham, North Carolina: Duke University Press, 2004).

Grochala, S. *The Contemporary Political Play: Rethinking Dramaturgical Structure* (London: Bloomsbury Methuen, 2017).

Healy, S. *Forty Years On: The Funding Conundrum at The Finborough*, Comparative Drama, Volume 56, Issue 1: *London's Theatre: Places, Communities, Futures* pp. 179–198, eds: Knapper, D. O'Thomas, M, Derbyshire, H and Holden, N. (Michigan. Western Michigan University Press, 2022).

Jeffreys, S. *Playwriting: Structure, Character, How and What to Write* (London: NHB, 2019).

Lang, T. *Essential Dramaturgy: The Mindset and Skillset* (London: Routledge, 2017).

Luckhurst, M. *Dramaturgy: A Revolution in Theatre* (Cambridge: Cambridge University Press, 2006).

McKee, R. *Story: Substance, Structure, Style and the Principles of Screenwriting* (New York: Methuen, 1999)

Mitchell, K. *The Director's Craft: A Handbook for the Theatre* (London: Routledge, 2009).

Romanska, M. *The Routledge Companion to Dramaturgy* (London: Routledge, 2016).

Trencsényi, K. *Dramaturgy in the Making: A User's Guide for Theatre Practitioners by Katalin* (London: Bloomsbury, 2015).

Turner, C. Behrndt, S. *Dramaturgy and Performance* (London: Palgrave Macmillan, 2007).

Vogler, C. *The Writers Journey: Mythic Structure for Writers* (New York: Michael Weise, 2007).

Waters, S. *The Secret Life of Plays* (London: NHB, 2010).

Index

A
Abbey Theatre, Dublin 6, 51, 115
de Angelis, April 82
Áras Éanna Arts Centre, Inis Oírr, Ireland 94, 108
Aristotle 54, 55
Arts Council Northern Ireland 9
Arvon Centre – The Hurst, Shropshire 97
Ashcroft, Peggy 119
Atlantic Theatre 5
Aukin, David 24
Ayckbourne, Alan 10, 40

B
Badham, Van 128
Barnes, Ben 6
BBC 15, 29
Behan, Brendan 24
Bell, Lian 115
Bell, Suzanne xi, xv
Billington, Michael 82
Birkbeck University, London 17
Bolton, Jacqueline 1, 6
Bourdieu, Pierre 112–114, 119
Brecht, Bertolt 55
Burns, Nica 122
Bush Theatre, London 38
Butler, Leo 65
Butterworth, Jez 24

C
Campbell, Chris xv, 3, 5, 6, 11, 14, 17, 19, 23, 24, 44, 52, 133
Carr, Marina 82
Chambers, Colin 22
Churchill, Caryl 157
Coel, Michaela 37
Cory, Alexandra 82
Criterion New Writing Programme 31, 32, 54, 79
Culleton, Jim 13

D
Dennis, Gill xv, 136
Devine, George 20, 24, 28, 30, 109, 119
Devine, Harriet xv, 20–22, 24, 110, 121
Dramaturges Network 63
Dublin Fringe 12
Dunn, Nell 106

E
Edgar, David 136, 159
English Touring Theatre 64

F
Farquhar, Simon xv, 68–74
Faye, Jimmy 15
Finborough Forum 82
Finborough Theatre i, xv, 18, 29, 43, 82, 122–130
Fishamble 12, 13, 23, 29
Fisher, Mark 55
Fortune Theatre, London 84
Fowler, Tommo xv, 62–63, 65
Frankcom, Sarah 19
Friel, Brian 25
Friel, Judy 6

G
Gaskill, William (Bill) 21, 24
Ginistrelle Artists' Residency, Assisi, Italy 98
von Goethe, Johann Wolfgang 55
Goetschius, Geoge 101
Glasgow University 17
Globe Theatre 88
Goddard, Lynette 82
Goldsmiths' University, London 17
Graham, James 37, 82, 123
Gregory, William xv, 51
Graeae Theatre Co. 117
Greig, David 40

H

Hanson, Barry 22
Haire, Wilson John 25
Hare, David 22, 24
Harris, Zinnie 40
Hayes, Rhys xv
Hampton, Christopher 22, 24
Healy, Sue i, 18
Heaney, Seamus 23
Hebditch, Fleur xv, 2, 4, 6, 10, 15, 23, 52, 61, 65, 133
Heinrich Boell Cottage, Ireland 95
Hewitt, John 23, 25
Holmes, Mark xv
Howarth, Donald xv, 22, 25, 60, 76, 101
Hynes, Garry 82

I

Irish Theatre Institute 12
Ireland, David 82

J

Jeffreys, Stephen xv, 136, 157, 159, 160
Jellicoe, Ann 22, 24
Johnstone, Keith 22
Joint Stock Theatre Company 24

K

Kane, Sarah 24
Kenyan, Mel 82
Kidd, Robert 22
King, Dawn 123
Kirkwood, Lucy 153
Kostick, Gavin xv, 12, 13, 19, 23, 24, 25, 38, 61, 65, 114, 115, 119

L

Leeds Conservatoire 17, 64
Lehmann, Hans-Thies 56
Lessing, Gotthold Ephraim 55
Lewenstein, Oscar 24, 25
Lir Academy, Dublin 13, 17, 23
Little, Ruth 19
Littlewood, Joan 111
LondonPlaywrightsBlog.com 29
Longley, Michael 23
Lustgarten, Anders 82
Lyric Theatre, Belfast 4, 9, 15, 40, 114, 129

M

Mac Conghail, Fiach 115
Mac Intyre, Tom 25
McDonagh, Martin 24, 37, 123
McKeon, Belinda 115
McPherson, Neil xv, 83, 123
Mairs, Rebecca xv, 4, 6, 9, 15, 16, 22, 23, 25, 40, 52, 61, 65, 90, 108, 114, 119, 129, 131, 136
Manhattan Theatre Club 5
Manzoni, Alessandro 55
Miles-Wildin, Nickie xv, 117–119
Mitchell, Katie 11
Mosse, Greg xv, 16, 54

N

Nasr, Carmen xv, 82
National Theatre, London 11, 14, 20, 29, 64
Neilson, Anthony 123
Nolan, Jim xv, 90
Northern Ireland Screen 15

O

O'Brien, Edna 24
Old Vic Theatre, London 57
Olivier, Laurence 20
Osborne, John 20, 24

P

Page, Anthony 76
Prebble, Lucy 24, 72

Q

Queen's University, Belfast 15

R

Ravenhill, Mark 78, 123
Rebellato, Dan 82
Richardson, Tony 130
Rickson, Ian 41, 72
Royal Court Theatre, London 3, 11, 14, 19, 20, 23, 24, 29, 30, 40, 41, 44, 51, 64, 68–72, 76, 78, 80, 82, 121, 133
Royal Exchange Theatre, Manchester xi, 19
Royal Shakespeare Company 22

S

Scanlan, Eva 13
Shakespeare & Co., Tumbleweed Residency, Paris 101
Sheffield Theatre 63
Shelley, Philip 82
Sierz, Aleks 82
Slattne, Hannah 23
Soho Theatre 70
Sophocles 55
Stafford-Clark, Max 24, 153
Steiger, Nina 70
Stephen Joseph Theatre, Scarborough 2, 10, 15
Stephens, Simon xv, 14, 19, 23, 24, 37, 38, 40, 52, 60, 61, 65, 67, 72, 78, 82, 107
Streep, Meryl 115

T

Theatre Royal, Stratford East, London 111
Tieck, Ludwig 55
Traverse Theatre, Edinburgh 40
tucker green, debbie 157
Tynan, Ken 20, 24
Tyn-y-Pant, Powys, Wales 92, 108
Tyrone Guthrie Centre, Ireland 91, 96, 100

V

Vaughan, Megan 82

W

Wade, Laura 123
Waller-Bridge, Phoebe 37, 38
Wasserberg, Kate 122
Watham, Claude 77
Weisz, Rachel 122
Whitehead, Edward (Ted) 76, 77
Whybrow, Graham xv, 19, 21, 23, 24, 41, 67, 71–74, 136, 153, 166–167
Wildridge, Ella 40
Wood, Alexandra 128

Y

Yaddo 108
Young Vic Theatre 64

For Product Safety Concerns and Information please contact our EU representative GPSR@taylorandfrancis.com
Taylor & Francis Verlag GmbH, Kaufingerstraße 24, 80331 München, Germany

www.ingramcontent.com/pod-product-compliance
Lightning Source LLC
Chambersburg PA
CBHW080411300426
44113CB00015B/2473